GED Math Preparation 2018

GED Test Review Workbook Team

FREE Test Taking Tips DVD Offer

To help us better serve you, we have developed a Test Taking Tips DVD that we would like to give you for FREE. **This DVD covers world-class test taking tips that you can use to be even more successful when you are taking your test.**

All that we ask is that you email us your feedback about your study guide. Please let us know what you thought about it – whether that is good, bad or indifferent.

To get your **FREE Test Taking Tips DVD**, email freedvd@studyguideteam.com with "FREE DVD" in the subject line and the following information in the body of the email:

> a. The title of your study guide.
>
> b. Your product rating on a scale of 1-5, with 5 being the highest rating.
>
> c. Your feedback about the study guide. What did you think of it?
>
> d. Your full name and shipping address to send your free DVD.

If you have any questions or concerns, please don't hesitate to contact us at freedvd@studyguideteam.com.

Thanks again!

Table of Contents

Quick Overview

As you draw closer to taking your exam, effective preparation becomes more and more important. Thankfully, you have this study guide to help you get ready. Use this guide to help keep your studying on track and refer to it often.

This study guide contains several key sections that will help you be successful on your exam. The guide contains tips for what you should do the night before and the day of the test. Also included are test-taking tips. Knowing the right information is not always enough. Many well-prepared test takers struggle with exams. These tips will help equip you to accurately read, assess, and answer test questions.

A large part of the guide is devoted to showing you what content to expect on the exam and to helping you better understand that content. Near the end of this guide is a practice test so that you can see how well you have grasped the content. Then, answer explanations are provided so that you can understand why you missed certain questions.

Don't try to cram the night before you take your exam. This is not a wise strategy for a few reasons. First, your retention of the information will be low. Your time would be better used by reviewing information you already know rather than trying to learn a lot of new information. Second, you will likely become stressed as you try to gain a large amount of knowledge in a short amount of time. Third, you will be depriving yourself of sleep. So be sure to go to bed at a reasonable time the night before. Being well-rested helps you focus and remain calm.

Be sure to eat a substantial breakfast the morning of the exam. If you are taking the exam in the afternoon, be sure to have a good lunch as well. Being hungry is distracting and can make it difficult to focus. You have hopefully spent lots of time preparing for the exam. Don't let an empty stomach get in the way of success!

When travelling to the testing center, leave earlier than needed. That way, you have a buffer in case you experience any delays. This will help you remain calm and will keep you from missing your appointment time at the testing center.

Be sure to pace yourself during the exam. Don't try to rush through the exam. There is no need to risk performing poorly on the exam just so you can leave the testing center early. Allow yourself to use all of the allotted time if needed.

Remain positive while taking the exam even if you feel like you are performing poorly. Thinking about the content you should have mastered will not help you perform better on the exam.

Once the exam is complete, take some time to relax. Even if you feel that you need to take the exam again, you will be well served by some down time before you begin studying again. It's often easier to convince yourself to study if you know that it will come with a reward!

Test-Taking Strategies

1. Predicting the Answer

When you feel confident in your preparation for a multiple-choice test, try predicting the answer before reading the answer choices. This is especially useful on questions that test objective factual knowledge or that ask you to fill in a blank. By predicting the answer before reading the available choices, you eliminate the possibility that you will be distracted or led astray by an incorrect answer choice. You will feel more confident in your selection if you read the question, predict the answer, and then find your prediction among the answer choices. After using this strategy, be sure to still read all of the answer choices carefully and completely. If you feel unprepared, you should not attempt to predict the answers. This would be a waste of time and an opportunity for your mind to wander in the wrong direction.

2. Reading the Whole Question

Too often, test takers scan a multiple-choice question, recognize a few familiar words, and immediately jump to the answer choices. Test authors are aware of this common impatience, and they will sometimes prey upon it. For instance, a test author might subtly turn the question into a negative, or he or she might redirect the focus of the question right at the end. The only way to avoid falling into these traps is to read the entirety of the question carefully before reading the answer choices.

3. Looking for Wrong Answers

Long and complicated multiple-choice questions can be intimidating. One way to simplify a difficult multiple-choice question is to eliminate all of the answer choices that are clearly wrong. In most sets of answers, there will be at least one selection that can be dismissed right away. If the test is administered on paper, the test taker could draw a line through it to indicate that it may be ignored; otherwise, the test taker will have to perform this operation mentally or on scratch paper. In either case, once the obviously incorrect answers have been eliminated, the remaining choices may be considered. Sometimes identifying the clearly wrong answers will give the test taker some information about the correct answer. For instance, if one of the remaining answer choices is a direct opposite of one of the eliminated answer choices, it may well be the correct answer. The opposite of obviously wrong is obviously right! Of course, this is not always the case. Some answers are obviously incorrect simply because they are irrelevant to the question being asked. Still, identifying and eliminating some incorrect answer choices is a good way to simplify a multiple-choice question.

4. Don't Overanalyze

Anxious test takers often overanalyze questions. When you are nervous, your brain will often run wild, causing you to make associations and discover clues that don't actually exist. If you feel that this may be a problem for you, do whatever you can to slow down during the test. Try taking a deep breath or counting to ten. As you read and consider the question, restrict yourself to the particular words used by the author. Avoid thought tangents about what the author *really* meant, or what he or she was *trying* to say. The only things that matter on a multiple-choice test are the words that are actually in the question. You must avoid reading too much into a multiple-choice question, or supposing that the writer meant something other than what he or she wrote.

5. No Need for Panic

It is wise to learn as many strategies as possible before taking a multiple-choice test, but it is likely that you will come across a few questions for which you simply don't know the answer. In this situation, avoid panicking. Because most multiple-choice tests include dozens of questions, the relative value of a single wrong answer is small. Moreover, your failure on one question has no effect on your success elsewhere on the test. As much as possible, you should compartmentalize each question on a multiple-choice test. In other words, you should not allow your feelings about one question to affect your success on the others. When you find a question that you either don't understand or don't know how to answer, just take a deep breath and do your best. Read the entire question slowly and carefully. Try rephrasing the question a couple of different ways. Then, read all of the answer choices carefully. After eliminating obviously wrong answers, make a selection and move on to the next question.

6. Confusing Answer Choices

When working on a difficult multiple-choice question, there may be a tendency to focus on the answer choices that are the easiest to understand. Many people, whether consciously or not, gravitate to the answer choices that require the least concentration, knowledge, and memory. This is a mistake. When you come across an answer choice that is confusing, you should give it extra attention. A question might be confusing because you do not know the subject matter to which it refers. If this is the case, don't eliminate the answer before you have affirmatively settled on another. When you come across an answer choice of this type, set it aside as you look at the remaining choices. If you can confidently assert that one of the other choices is correct, you can leave the confusing answer aside. Otherwise, you will need to take a moment to try to better understand the confusing answer choice. Rephrasing is one way to tease out the sense of a confusing answer choice.

7. Your First Instinct

Many people struggle with multiple-choice tests because they overthink the questions. If you have studied sufficiently for the test, you should be prepared to trust your first instinct once you have carefully and completely read the question and all of the answer choices. There is a great deal of research suggesting that the mind can come to the correct conclusion very quickly once it has obtained all of the relevant information. At times, it may seem to you as if your intuition is working faster even than your reasoning mind. This may in fact be true. The knowledge you obtain while studying may be retrieved from your subconscious before you have a chance to work out the associations that support it. Verify your instinct by working out the reasons that it should be trusted.

8. Key Words

Many test takers struggle with multiple-choice questions because they have poor reading comprehension skills. Quickly reading and understanding a multiple-choice question requires a mixture of skill and experience. To help with this, try jotting down a few key words and phrases on a piece of scrap paper. Doing this concentrates the process of reading and forces the mind to weigh the relative importance of the question's parts. In selecting words and phrases to write down, the test taker thinks about the question more deeply and carefully. This is especially true for multiple-choice questions that are preceded by a long prompt.

9. Subtle Negatives

One of the oldest tricks in the multiple-choice test writer's book is to subtly reverse the meaning of a question with a word like *not* or *except*. If you are not paying attention to each word in the question, you can easily be led astray by this trick. For instance, a common question format is, "Which of the following is...?" Obviously, if the question instead is, "Which of the following is not...?," then the answer will be quite different. Even worse, the test makers are aware of the potential for this mistake and will include one answer choice that would be correct if the question were not negated or reversed. A test taker who misses the reversal will find what he or she believes to be a correct answer and will be so confident that he or she will fail to reread the question and discover the original error. The only way to avoid this is to practice a wide variety of multiple-choice questions and to pay close attention to each and every word.

10. Reading Every Answer Choice

It may seem obvious, but you should always read every one of the answer choices! Too many test takers fall into the habit of scanning the question and assuming that they understand the question because they recognize a few key words. From there, they pick the first answer choice that answers the question they believe they have read. Test takers who read all of the answer choices might discover that one of the latter answer choices is actually *more* correct. Moreover, reading all of the answer choices can remind you of facts related to the question that can help you arrive at the correct answer. Sometimes, a misstatement or incorrect detail in one of the latter answer choices will trigger your memory of the subject and will enable you to find the right answer. Failing to read all of the answer choices is like not reading all of the items on a restaurant menu: you might miss out on the perfect choice.

11. Spot the Hedges

One of the keys to success on multiple-choice tests is paying close attention to every word. This is never more true than with words like *almost*, *most*, *some*, and *sometimes*. These words are called "hedges" because they indicate that a statement is not totally true or not true in every place and time. An absolute statement will contain no hedges, but in many subjects, like literature and history, the answers are not always straightforward or absolute. There are always exceptions to the rules in these subjects. For this reason, you should favor those multiple-choice questions that contain hedging language. The presence of qualifying words indicates that the author is taking special care with his or her words, which is certainly important when composing the right answer. After all, there are many ways to be wrong, but there is only one way to be right! For this reason, it is wise to avoid answers that are absolute when taking a multiple-choice test. An absolute answer is one that says things are either all one way or all another. They often include words like *every*, *always*, *best*, and *never*. If you are taking a multiple-choice test in a subject that doesn't lend itself to absolute answers, be on your guard if you see any of these words.

12. Long Answers

In many subject areas, the answers are not simple. As already mentioned, the right answer often requires hedges. Another common feature of the answers to a complex or subjective question are qualifying clauses, which are groups of words that subtly modify the meaning of the sentence. If the question or answer choice describes a rule to which there are exceptions or the subject matter is complicated, ambiguous, or confusing, the correct answer will require many words in order to be expressed clearly and accurately. In essence, you should not be deterred by answer choices that seem excessively long. Oftentimes, the author of the text will not be able to write the correct answer without offering some qualifications and modifications. Your job is to read the answer choices thoroughly and completely and to select the one that most accurately and precisely answers the question.

13. Restating to Understand

Sometimes, a question on a multiple-choice test is difficult not because of what it asks but because of how it is written. If this is the case, restate the question or answer choice in different words. This process serves a couple of important purposes. First, it forces you to concentrate on the core of the question. In order to rephrase the question accurately, you have to understand it well. Rephrasing the question will concentrate your mind on the key words and ideas. Second, it will present the information to your mind in a fresh way. This process may trigger your memory and render some useful scrap of information picked up while studying.

14. True Statements

Sometimes an answer choice will be true in itself, but it does not answer the question. This is one of the main reasons why it is essential to read the question carefully and completely before proceeding to the answer choices. Too often, test takers skip ahead to the answer choices and look for true statements. Having found one of these, they are content to select it without reference to the question above. Obviously, this provides an easy way for test makers to play tricks. The savvy test taker will always read the entire question before turning to the answer choices. Then, having settled on a correct answer choice, he or she will refer to the original question and ensure that the selected answer is relevant. The mistake of choosing a correct-but-irrelevant answer choice is especially common on questions related to specific pieces of objective knowledge, like historical or scientific facts. A prepared test taker will have a wealth of factual knowledge at his or her disposal, and should not be careless in its application.

15. No Patterns

One of the more dangerous ideas that circulates about multiple-choice tests is that the correct answers tend to fall into patterns. These erroneous ideas range from a belief that B and C are the most common right answers, to the idea that an unprepared test-taker should answer "A-B-A-C-A-D-A-B-A." It cannot be emphasized enough that pattern-seeking of this type is exactly the WRONG way to approach a multiple-choice test. To begin with, it is highly unlikely that the test maker will plot the correct answers according to some predetermined pattern. The questions are scrambled and delivered in a random order. Furthermore, even if the test maker was following a pattern in the assignation of correct answers, there is no reason why the test taker would know which pattern he or she was using. Any attempt to discern a pattern in the answer choices is a waste of time and a distraction from the real work of taking the test. A test taker would be much better served by extra preparation before the test than by reliance on a pattern in the answers.

FREE DVD OFFER

Don't forget that doing well on your exam includes both understanding the test content and understanding how to use what you know to do well on the test. We offer a completely FREE Test Taking Tips DVD that covers world class test taking tips that you can use to be even more successful when you are taking your test.

All that we ask is that you email us your feedback about your study guide. To get your **FREE Test Taking Tips DVD**, email freedvd@studyguideteam.com with "FREE DVD" in the subject line and the following information in the body of the email:

- The title of your study guide.
- Your product rating on a scale of 1-5, with 5 being the highest rating.
- Your feedback about the study guide. What did you think of it?
- Your full name and shipping address to send your free DVD.

Introduction to the GED

Function of the Test

The General Education Development (GED) test is an exam developed and administered by the GED Testing Service, a joint venture of the American Council on Education and Pearson VUE. The GED offers those without a high school diploma the chance to earn a high school equivalency credential by evaluating their knowledge of core high school subjects. In 2014, the test was updated to become computer-based only and to align with current high school graduation standards.

The GED is the only nationally recognized high school equivalency credential, and GED test takers represent a wide age group with diverse goals. Generally, the GED is appropriate for people who did not graduate from high school but who wish to pursue advancement in their career and/or education. According to MyGED, approximately 98% of U.S. colleges and universities accept a GED as the equivalent of a high school diploma (other schools may require additional preparation courses in addition to a passing GED score in order to be considered for admission). Over 20 million adults have earned GED credentials, and the latest reported pass rates for the 2014 GED are around 60%.

Test Administration

GED tests are widely offered throughout the United States and Canada, although jurisdictions (state, province, etc.) may vary in terms of things like pricing, scheduling, and test rules. For international students and US military, international testing options are also available. Official GED Testing Centers are often operated by community colleges, adult education centers, and local school boards; GED Testing Service offers a comprehensive search of nearby test centers.

Keeping in mind that rules may vary between jurisdictions, all tests are administered in-person and taken on a computer. Tests are scheduled throughout the year; refer to local testing centers for available test times. Generally, test takers are able to take any test module three times without any restrictions on retesting. However, after three failed attempts, testers must wait a minimum of 60 days to retake the test. GED testing centers can also offer accommodations for students with disabilities, such as additional test time or Braille format tests. The GED may also be offered in Spanish or in French (verify availability with local testing centers). (http://www.gedtestingservice.com/testers/mygedfaqs)

Test Format

The GED consists of four sections, or modules: Mathematical Reasoning, Science, Social Studies, and Reasoning Through Language Arts. Although the complete test is offered together, it is not necessary to take all four modules at once. Test subjects vary in length:

Subject	Time	Topics
Math	115 minutes	Quantitative and algebraic problem solving; data analysis of charts, graphs, and tables; geometry
Science	90 minutes	Life science, physical science, earth and space science
Social Studies	70 minutes	Civics and government, U.S. history, economics, world geography
Reasoning Through Language Arts	150 minutes	Ability to closely read, comprehend, and edit written text; ability to write clearly

A ten-minute break is given between each module.

On the testing day, test takers are not permitted to eat, drink, smoke, or use their cell phones during the test. Test takers are permitted to bring a handheld calculator (TI-30XS Multiview Scientific Calculator) to the test; testing centers will not provide handheld calculators, although an on-screen calculator will be available on the computer. Students will also be provided with three erasable note boards to use during the test.

Scoring

Because the GED is now a computer-based test, scores will be available on MyGED within 24 hours of completing the test. The four modules of the GED are scored on a scale of 100–200. In order to earn high school equivalency, it is necessary to achieve a passing score on all of the four modules, and scores cannot be made up between modules—that is, a high score on one subject cannot be used to compensate for a low score on another subject. Scores are divided into four ranges:

> 1. A score lower than 145 points earns a score of "Not Passing." It is necessary to retake the test to earn high school equivalency.

> 2. A score at or higher than 145 points earns "GED Passing Score/High School Equivalency."

> 3. A score of 165-175 is deemed "GED College Ready." This designation advises colleges and universities that the test taker is ready to begin a degree program without further placement testing or preparation courses (policies vary among schools).

> 4. A score over 175 earns the test taker "GED College Ready + Credit." For some institutions, a score at this level allows the GED graduate to earn college credit for certain courses (policies vary among schools).

Recent/Future Developments

The 2014 GED is the newest version of the test. It was updated to reflect current high school education standards. Initial score results reflected lower pass rates on the 2014 GED compared to earlier versions of the test, so GED Testing Service adjusted score ranges to compensate for the increased difficulty of the exam.

Mathematical Reasoning

Number Operations/Number Sense

Numbers and Their Classifications

Rational numbers are any number that can be written as a fraction or ratio. Within the set of rational numbers, several subsets exist that are referenced throughout the mathematics topics. Counting numbers are the first numbers learned as a child. Counting numbers consist of 1,2,3,4, and so on. Whole numbers include all counting numbers and zero (0,1,2,3,4,…). Integers include counting numbers, their opposites, and zero (…,-3,-2,-1,0,1,2,3,…). Rational numbers are inclusive of integers, fractions, and decimals that terminate, or end (1.7, 0.04213) or repeat (0.136$\overline{5}$).

A number line typically consists of integers (…3,2,1,0,-1,-2,-3…), and is used to visually represent the value of a rational number. Each rational number has a distinct position on the line determined by comparing its value with the displayed values on the line. For example, if plotting -1.5 on the number line below, it is necessary to recognize that the value of -1.5 is .5 less than -1 and .5 greater than -2. Therefore, -1.5 is plotted halfway between -1 and -2.

The number system that is used consists of only ten different digits or characters. However, this system is used to represent an infinite number of values. The place value system makes this infinite number of values possible. The position in which a digit is written corresponds to a given value. Starting from the decimal point (which is implied, if not physically present), each subsequent place value to the left represents a value greater than the one before it. Conversely, starting from the decimal point, each subsequent place value to the right represents a value less than the one before it.

The names for the place values to the left of the decimal point are as follows:

…	Billions	Hundred-Millions	Ten-Millions	Millions	Hundred-Thousands	Ten-Thousands	Thousands	Hundreds	Tens	Ones

*Note that this table can be extended infinitely further to the left.

The names for the place values to the right of the decimal point are as follows:

Decimal Point (.)	Tenths	Hundredths	Thousandths	Ten-Thousandths	…

*Note that this table can be extended infinitely further to the right.

When given a multi-digit number, the value of each digit depends on its place value. Consider the number 682,174.953. Referring to the chart above, it can be determined that the digit 8 is in the ten-thousands place. It is in the fifth place to the left of the decimal point. Its value is 8 ten-thousands or 80,000. The digit 5 is two places to the right of the decimal point. Therefore, the digit 5 is in the hundredths place. Its value is 5 hundredths or $\frac{5}{100}$ (equivalent to .05).

In accordance with the base-10 system, the value of a digit increases by a factor of ten each place it moves to the left. For example, consider the number 7. Moving the digit one place to the left (70), increases its value by a factor of 10 ($7 \times 10 = 70$). Moving the digit two places to the left (700) increases its value by a factor of 10 twice ($7 \times 10 \times 10 = 700$). Moving the digit three places to the left (7,000) increases its value by a factor of 10 three times ($7 \times 10 \times 10 \times 10 = 7,000$), and so on.

Conversely, the value of a digit decreases by a factor of ten each place it moves to the right. (Note that multiplying by $\frac{1}{10}$ is equivalent to dividing by 10). For example, consider the number 40. Moving the digit one place to the right (4) decreases its value by a factor of 10 ($40 \div 10 = 4$). Moving the digit two places to the right (0.4), decreases its value by a factor of 10 twice ($40 \div 10 \div 10 = 0.4$) or ($40 \times \frac{1}{10} \times \frac{1}{10} = 0.4$). Moving the digit three places to the right (0.04) decreases its value by a factor of 10 three times ($40 \div 10 \div 10 \div 10 = 0.04$) or ($40 \times \frac{1}{10} \times \frac{1}{10} \times \frac{1}{10} = 0.04$), and so on.

Rounding
Rounding numbers changes the given number to a simpler and less accurate number than the exact given number. Rounding allows for easier calculations which estimate the results of using the exact given number. The accuracy of the estimate and ease of use depends on the place value to which the number is rounded. Rounding numbers consists of:

- Determining what place value the number is being rounded to
- Examining the digit to the right of the desired place value to decide whether to round up or keep the digit
- Replacing all digits to the right of the desired place value with zeros

To round 746,311 to the nearest ten thousands, the digit in the ten thousands place should be located first. In this case, this digit is 4 (746,311). Then, the digit to its right is examined. If this digit is 5 or greater, the number will be rounded up by increasing the digit in the desired place by one. If the digit to the right of the place value being rounded is 4 or less, the number will be kept the same. For the given example, the digit being examined is a 6, which means that the number will be rounded up by increasing the digit to the left by one. Therefore, the digit 4 is changed to a 5. Finally, to write the rounded number, any digits to the left of the place value being rounded remain the same and any to its right are replaced with zeros. For the given example, rounding 746,311 to the nearest ten thousand will produce 750,000. To round 746,311 to the nearest hundred, the digit to the right of the three in the hundreds place is examined to determine whether to round up or keep the same number. In this case, that digit is a one, so the number will be kept the same and any digits to its right will be replaced with zeros. The resulting rounded number is 746,300.

Rounding place values to the right of the decimal follows the same procedure, but digits being replaced by zeros can simply be dropped. To round 3.752891 to the nearest thousandth, the desired place value is located (3.752891) and the digit to the right is examined. In this case, the digit 8 indicates that the number will be rounded up, and the 2 in the thousandths place will increase to a 3. Rounding up and replacing the digits to the right of the thousandths place produces 3.753000 which is equivalent to 3.753. Therefore, the zeros are not necessary and the rounded number should be written as 3.753.

When rounding up, if the digit to be increased is a 9, the digit to its left is increased by 1 and the digit in the desired place value is changed to a zero. For example, the number 1,598 rounded to the nearest ten is 1,600. Another example shows the number 43.72961 rounded to the nearest thousandth is 43.730 or 43.73.

Operations

Addition combines two quantities together. With whole numbers, this is taking two sets of things and merging them into one, then counting the result. For example, 4 + 3 = 7. When adding numbers, the order does not matter: 3 + 4 = 7, also. Longer lists of whole numbers can also be added together. The result of adding numbers is called the *sum*.

With fractions, the number on top is the *numerator*, and the number on the bottom is the *denominator*. To add fractions, the denominator must be the same—a *common denominator*. To find a common denominator, the existing numbers on the bottom must be considered, and the lowest number they will both multiply into must be determined. Consider the following equation:

$$\frac{1}{3} + \frac{5}{6} = ?$$

The numbers 3 and 6 both multiply into 6. Three can be multiplied by 2, and 6 can be multiplied by 1. The top and bottom of each fraction must be multiplied by the same number. Then, the numerators are added together to get a new numerator. The following equation is the result:

$$\frac{1}{3} + \frac{5}{6} = \frac{2}{6} + \frac{5}{6} = \frac{7}{6}$$

Subtraction is taking one quantity away from another, so it is the opposite of addition. The expression 4 − 3 means taking 3 away from 4. So, 4 − 3 = 1. In this case, the order matters, since it entails taking one quantity away from the other, rather than just putting two quantities together. The result of subtraction is also called the *difference*.

To subtract fractions, the denominator must be the same. Then, subtract the numerators together to get a new numerator. Here is an example:

$$\frac{1}{3} - \frac{5}{6} = \frac{2}{6} - \frac{5}{6} = \frac{-3}{6} = -\frac{1}{2}$$

Multiplication is a kind of repeated addition. The expression 4 × 5 is taking four sets, each of them having five things in them, and putting them all together. That means $4 \times 5 = 5 + 5 + 5 + 5 = 20$. As with addition, the order of the numbers does not matter. The result of a multiplication problem is called the *product.*

To multiply fractions, the numerators are multiplied to get the new numerator, and the denominators are multiplied to get the new denominator:

$$\frac{1}{3} \times \frac{5}{6} = \frac{1 \times 5}{3 \times 6} = \frac{5}{18}$$

When multiplying fractions, common factors can *cancel* or *divide into one another*, when factors that appear in the numerator of one fraction and the denominator of the other fraction. Here is an example:

$$\frac{1}{3} \times \frac{9}{8} = \frac{1}{1} \times \frac{3}{8} = 1 \times \frac{3}{8} = \frac{3}{8}$$

The numbers 3 and 9 have a common factor of 3, so that factor can be divided out.

Division is the opposite of multiplication. With whole numbers, it means splitting up one number into sets of equal size. For example, $16 \div 8$ is the number of sets of eight things that can be made out of sixteen things. Thus, $16 \div 8 = 2$. As with subtraction, the order of the numbers will make a difference, here. The answer to a division problem is called the *quotient*, while the number in front of the division sign is called the *dividend* and the number behind the division sign is called the *divisor*.

To divide fractions, the first fraction must be multiplied with the reciprocal of the second fraction. The *reciprocal* of the fraction $\frac{x}{y}$ is the fraction $\frac{y}{x}$. Here is an example:

$$\frac{1}{3} \div \frac{5}{6} = \frac{1}{3} \times \frac{6}{5} = \frac{6}{15} = \frac{2}{5}$$

The value of a fraction does not change if multiplying or dividing both the numerator and the denominator by the same number (other than 0). In other words, $\frac{x}{y} = \frac{a \times x}{a \times y} = \frac{x \div a}{y \div a}$, as long as a is not 0. This means that $\frac{2}{5} = \frac{4}{10}$, for example. If x and y are integers that have no common factors, then the fraction is said to be *simplified*. This means $\frac{2}{5}$ is simplified, but $\frac{4}{10}$ is not.

Often when working with fractions, the fractions need to be rewritten so that they all share a single denominator—this is called finding a *common denominator* for the fractions. Using two fractions, $\frac{a}{b}$ and $\frac{c}{d}$, the numerator and denominator of the left fraction can be multiplied by d, while the numerator and denominator of the right fraction can be multiplied by b. This provides the fractions $\frac{a \times d}{b \times d}$ and $\frac{c \times b}{d \times b}$ with the common denominator $b \times d$.

A fraction whose numerator is smaller than its denominator is called a *proper fraction*. A fraction whose numerator is bigger than its denominator is called an *improper fraction*. These numbers can be rewritten as a combination of integers and fractions, called a *mixed number*. For example, $\frac{6}{5} = \frac{5}{5} + \frac{1}{5} = 1 + \frac{1}{5}$, and can be written as $1\frac{1}{5}$.

Estimation is finding a value that is close to a solution but is not the exact answer. For example, if there are values in the thousands to be multiplied, then each value can be estimated to the nearest thousand and the calculation performed. This value provides an approximate solution that can be determined very quickly.

Sometimes when multiplying numbers, the result can be estimated by *rounding*. For example, to estimate the value of 11.2×2.01, each number can be rounded to the nearest integer. This will yield a result of 22.

The *decimal system* is a way of writing out numbers that uses ten different numerals: 0, 1, 2, 3, 4, 5, 6, 7, 8, and 9. This is also called a "base ten" or "base 10" system. Other bases are also used. For example, computers work with a base of 2. This means they only use the numerals 0 and 1.

The *decimal place* denotes how far to the right of the decimal point a numeral is. The first digit to the right of the decimal point is in the *tenths* place. The next is the *hundredths*. The third is the *thousandths*.

So, 3.142 has a 1 in the tenths place, a 4 in the hundredths place, and a 2 in the thousandths place.

The *decimal point* is a period used to separate the *ones* place from the *tenths* place when writing out a number as a decimal.

A *decimal number* is a number written out with a decimal point instead of as a fraction, for example, 1.25 instead of $\frac{5}{4}$. Depending on the situation, it can sometimes be easier to work with fractions and sometimes easier to work with decimal numbers.

A decimal number is *terminating* if it stops at some point. It is called *repeating* if it never stops, but repeats a pattern over and over. It is important to note that every rational number can be written as a terminating decimal or as a repeating decimal.

To add decimal numbers, each number in columns needs to be lined up by the decimal point. For each number being added, the zeros to the right of the last number need to be filled in so that each of the numbers has the same number of places to the right of the decimal. Then, the columns can be added together. Here is an example of 2.45 + 1.3 + 8.891 written in column form:

$$2.450$$

$$1.300$$

$$+\ 8.891$$

Zeros have been added in the columns so that each number has the same number of places to the right of the decimal.

Added together, the correct answer is 12.641:

$$2.450$$

$$1.300$$

$$+\ 8.891$$

$$12.641$$

Subtracting decimal numbers is the same process as adding decimals. Here is 7.89 − 4.235 written in column form:

$$7.890$$

$$-\ 4.235$$

$$3.655$$

A zero has been added in the column so that each number has the same number of places to the right of the decimal.

Decimals can be multiplied as if there were no decimals points in the problem. For example, 0.5 x 1.25 can be rewritten and multiplied as 5 x 125, which equals 625.

The final answer will have the same number of decimal *points* as the total number of decimal *places* in the problem. The first number has one decimal place, and the second number has two decimal places. Therefore, the final answer will contain three decimal places:

0.5 x 1.25 = 0.625

Dividing a decimal by a whole number entails using long division first by ignoring the decimal point. Then, the decimal point is moved the number of places given in the problem.

For example, $6.8 \div 4$ can be rewritten as $68 \div 4$, which is 17. There is one non-zero integer to the right of the decimal point, so the final solution would have one decimal place to the right of the solution. In this case, the solution is 1.7.

Dividing a decimal by another decimal requires changing the divisor to a whole number by moving its decimal point. The decimal place of the dividend should be moved by the same number of places as the divisor. Then, the problem is the same as dividing a decimal by a whole number.

For example, $5.72 \div 1.1$ has a divisor with one decimal point in the denominator. The expression can be rewritten as $57.2 \div 11$ by moving each number one decimal place to the right to eliminate the decimal. The long division can be completed as $572 \div 11$ with a result of 52. Since there is one non-zero integer to the right of the decimal point in the problem, the final solution is 5.2.

In another example, $8 \div 0.16$ has a divisor with two decimal points in the denominator. The expression can be rewritten as $800 \div 16$ by moving each number two decimal places to the right to eliminate the decimal in the divisor. The long division can be completed with a result of 50.

Algebra, Functions, and Patterns

Working With Positive and Negative Numbers
When adding integers and negative rational numbers, there are some basic rules to determine if the solution is negative or positive:

Adding two positive numbers results in a positive number: 3.3 + 4.8 = 8.1.

Adding two negative numbers results in a negative number: (-8) + (-6) = -14.

Adding one positive and one negative number requires taking the absolute values and finding the difference between them. Then, the sign of the number that has the higher absolute value for the final solution is used.

For example, (-9) + 11, has a difference of absolute values of 2. The final solution is 2 because 11 has the higher absolute value. Another example is 9 + (-11), which has a difference of absolute values of 2. The final solution is -2 because 11 has the higher absolute value.

When subtracting integers and negative rational numbers, one has to change the problem to adding the opposite and then apply the rules of addition.

Subtracting two positive numbers is the same as adding one positive and one negative number.

For example, 4.9 − 7.1 is the same as 4.9 + (-7.1). The solution is -2.2 since the absolute value of -7.1 is greater. Another example is 8.5 − 6.4 which is the same as 8.5 + (-6.4). The solution is 2.1 since the absolute value of 8.5 is greater.

Subtracting a positive number from a negative number results in negative value.

For example, $(-12) - 7$ is the same as $(-12) + (-7)$ with a solution of -19.

Subtracting a negative number from a positive number results in a positive value.

For example, $12 - (-7)$ is the same as $12 + 7$ with a solution of 19.

For multiplication and division of integers and rational numbers, if both numbers are positive or both numbers are negative, the result is a positive value.

For example, $(-1.7)(-4)$ has a solution of 6.8 since both numbers are negative values.

If one number is positive and another number is negative, the result is a negative value.

For example, $(-15)/5$ has a solution of -3 since there is one negative number.

Order of Operations

Exponents are shorthand for longer multiplications or divisions. The exponent is written to the upper right of a number. In the expression 2^3, the exponent is 3. The number with the exponent is called the *base*.

When the exponent is a whole number, it means to multiply the base by itself as many times as the number in the exponent. So, $2^3 = 2 \times 2 \times 2 = 8$.

If the exponent is a negative number, it means to take the reciprocal of the positive exponent:

$$2^{-3} = \frac{1}{2^3} = \frac{1}{8}$$

When the exponent is 0, the result is always 1: $2^0 = 1, 5^0 = 1$, and so on.

When the exponent is 2, the number is *squared*, and when the exponent is 3, it is *cubed*.

When working with longer expressions, parentheses are used to show the order in which the operations should be performed. Operations inside the parentheses should be completed first. Thus, $(3 - 1) \div 2$ means one should first subtract 1 from 3, and then divide that result by 2.

The *order of operations* gives an order for how a mathematical expression is to be simplified:

- Parentheses
- Exponents
- Multiplication
- Division
- Addition
- Subtraction

To help remember this, many students like to use the mnemonic PEMDAS. Some students associate this word with a phrase to help them, such as "Pirates Eat Many Donuts at Sea." Here is a quick example:

$$\text{Evaluate } 2^2 \times (3 - 1) \div 2 + 3.$$

$$\text{Parenthesis: } 2^2 \times 2 \div 2 + 3.$$

$$\text{Exponents: } 4 \times 2 \div 2 + 3$$

$$\text{Multiply: } 8 \div 2 + 3.$$

$$\text{Divide: } 4 + 3.$$

$$\text{Addition: } 7$$

Percentages, Ratios, and Proportions

The word *percent* comes from the Latin phrase for "per one hundred." A *percent* is a way of writing out a fraction. It is a fraction with a denominator of 100. Thus, $65\% = \frac{65}{100}$.

To convert a fraction to a percent, the denominator is written as 100. For example, $\frac{3}{5} = \frac{60}{100} = 60\%$.

In converting a percent to a fraction, the percent is written with a denominator of 100, and the result is simplified. For example, $30\% = \frac{30}{100} = \frac{3}{10}$.

The basic percent equation is the following:

$$\frac{is}{of} = \frac{\%}{100}$$

The placement of numbers in the equation depends on what the question asks.

Example 1
Find 40% of 80.

Basically, the problem is asking, "What is 40% of 80?" The 40% is the percent, and 80 is the number to find the percent "of." The equation is:

$$\frac{x}{80} = \frac{40}{100}$$

Solving the equation by cross-multiplication, the problem becomes 100x = 80(40). Solving for x gives the answer: x = 32.

Example 2
What percent of 100 is 20?

The 20 fills in the "is" portion, while 100 fills in the "of." The question asks for the percent, so that will be x, the unknown. The following equation is set up:

$$\frac{20}{100} = \frac{x}{100}$$

Cross-multiplying yields the equation 100x = 20(100). Solving for x gives the answer of 20%.

<u>Example 3</u>
30% of what number is 30?

The following equation uses the clues and numbers in the problem:

$$\frac{30}{x} = \frac{30}{100}$$

Cross-multiplying results in the equation 30(100) = 30x. Solving for x gives the answer x = 100.

A *ratio* compares the size of one group to the size of another. For example, there may be a room with 4 tables and 24 chairs. The ratio of tables to chairs is 4: 24. Such ratios behave like fractions in that both sides of the ratio by the same number can be multiplied or divided. Thus, the ratio 4:24 is the same as the ratio 2:12 and 1:6.

One quantity is *proportional* to another quantity if the first quantity is always some multiple of the second. For instance, the distance travelled in five hours is always five times to the speed as travelled. The distance is proportional to speed in this case.

One quantity is *inversely proportional* to another quantity if the first quantity is equal to some number divided by the second quantity. The time it takes to travel one hundred miles will be given by 100 divided by the speed travelled. The time is inversely proportional to the speed.

When dealing with word problems, there is no fixed series of steps to follow, but there are some general guidelines to use. It is important that the quantity that to be found is identified. Then, it can be determined how the given values can be used and manipulated to find the final answer.

<u>Example 1</u>
Jana wants to travel to visit Alice, who lives one hundred and fifty miles away. If she can drive at fifty miles per hour, how long will her trip take?

The quantity to find is the *time* of the trip. The time of a trip is given by the distance to travel divided by the speed to be traveled. The problem determines that the distance is one hundred and fifty miles, while the speed is fifty miles per hour. Thus, 150 divided by 50 is $150 \div 50 = 3$. Because *miles* and *miles per hour* are the units being divided, the miles cancel out. The result is 3 hours.

<u>Example 2</u>
Bernard wishes to paint a wall that measures twenty feet wide by eight feet high. It costs ten cents to paint one square foot. How much money will Bernard need for paint?

The final quantity to compute is the *cost* to paint the wall. This will be ten cents ($0.10) for each square foot of area needed to paint. The area to be painted is unknown, but the dimensions of the wall are given; thus, it can be calculated.

The dimensions of the wall are 20 feet wide and 8 feet high. Since the area of a rectangle is length multiplied by width, the area of the wall is 8 x 20 = 160 square feet. Multiplying 0.1 x 160 yields $16 as the cost of the paint.

To convert a fraction to a decimal, the numerator is divided by the denominator. For example, $\frac{3}{8}$ can be converted to a decimal by dividing 3 by 8 ($\frac{3}{8} = 0.375$). To convert a decimal to a fraction, the decimal point is dropped and the value is written as the numerator. The denominator is the place value farthest to the right with a digit other than zero. For example, to convert .48 to a fraction, the numerator is 48 and the denominator is 100 (the digit 8 is in the hundredths place). Therefore, .48 = $\frac{48}{100}$. Fractions should be written in the simplest form, or reduced. To reduce a fraction, the numerator and denominator are divided by the largest common factor. In the previous example, 48 and 100 are both divisible by 4. Dividing the numerator and denominator by 4 results in a reduced fraction of $\frac{12}{25}$.

To convert a decimal to a percent, the number is multiplied by 100. To convert .13 to a percent, .13 is multiplied by 100 to get 13 percent. To convert a fraction to a percent, the fraction is converted to a decimal and then multiplied by 100. For example, $\frac{1}{5}$ = .20 and .20 multiplied by 100 produces 20 percent.

To convert a percent to a decimal, the value is divided by 100. For example, 125 percent is equal to 1.25 ($\frac{125}{100}$). To convert a percent to a fraction, the percent sign is dropped and the value is written as the numerator with a denominator of 100. For example, 80% = $\frac{80}{100}$. This fraction can be reduced ($\frac{80}{100} = \frac{4}{5}$).

<u>Scientific Notation</u>
Scientific Notation is used to represent numbers that are either very small or very large. For example, the distance to the sun is approximately 150,000,000,000 meters. Instead of writing this number with so many zeros, it can be written in scientific notation as $1.5 * 10^{11}$ meters. The same is true for very small numbers, but the exponent becomes negative. If the mass of a human cell is 0.000000000001 kilograms, that measurement can be easily represented by $1.0 * 10^{-12}$ kilograms. In both situations, scientific notation makes the measurement easier to read and understand. Each number is translated to an expression with one digit in the tens place times an expression corresponding to the zeros.

When two measurements are given and both involve scientific notation, it is important to know how these interact with each other:

- In addition and subtraction, the exponent on the ten must be the same before any operations are performed on the numbers. For example, $(1.3 * 10^4) + (3.0 * 10^3)$ cannot be added until one of the exponents on the ten is changed. The $3.0 * 10^3$ can be changed to $0.3 * 10^4$, then the 1.3 and 0.3 can be added. The answer comes out to be $1.6 * 10^4$.

- For multiplication, the first numbers can be multiplied and then the exponents on the tens can be added. Once an answer is formed, it may have to be converted into scientific notation again depending on the change that occurred.

- The following is an example of multiplication with scientific notation:

$$(4.5 * 10^3) * (3.0 * 10^{-5}) = 13.5 * 10^{-2}$$

- Since this answer is not in scientific notation, the decimal is moved over to the left one unit, and 1 is added to the ten's exponent. This results in the final answer: $1.35 * 10^{-1}$.

- For division, the first numbers are divided, and the exponents on the tens are subtracted. Again, the answer may need to be converted into scientific notation form, depending on the type of changes that occurred during the problem.

- *Order of magnitude* relates to scientific notation and is the total count of powers of 10 in a number. For example, there are 6 orders of magnitude in 1,000,000. If a number is raised by an order of magnitude, it is multiplied times 10. Order of magnitude can be helpful in estimating results using very large or small numbers. An answer should make sense in terms of its order of magnitude.

- For example, if area is calculated using two dimensions with 6 orders of magnitude, because area involves multiplication, the answer should have around 12 orders of magnitude. Also, answers can be estimated by rounding to the largest place value in each number. For example, 5,493,302 * 2,523,100 can be estimated by 5 * 3 = 15 with 6 orders of magnitude.

Properties of Operations

Properties of operations exist that make calculations easier and solve problems for missing values. The following table summarizes commonly used properties of real numbers.

Property	Addition	Multiplication
Commutative	$a + b = b + a$	$a \times b = b \times a$
Associative	$(a + b) + c = a + (b + c)$	$(a \times b) \times c = a \times (bc)$
Identity	$a + 0 = a; 0 + a = a$	$a \times 1 = a; 1 \times a = a$
Inverse	$a + (-a) = 0$	$a \times \dfrac{1}{a} = 1; a \neq 0$
Distributive	$a(b + c) = ab + ac$	

The commutative property of addition states that the order in which numbers are added does not change the sum. Similarly, the commutative property of multiplication states that the order in which numbers are multiplied does not change the product. The associative property of addition and multiplication state that the grouping of numbers being added or multiplied does not change the sum or product, respectively. The commutative and associative properties are useful for performing calculations. For example, $(47 + 25) + 3$ is equivalent to $(47 + 3) + 25$, which is easier to calculate.

The identity property of addition states that adding zero to any number does not change its value. The identity property of multiplication states that multiplying a number by one does not change its value. The inverse property of addition states that the sum of a number and its opposite equals zero. Opposites are numbers that are the same with different signs (ex. 5 and -5; $-\frac{1}{2}$ and $\frac{1}{2}$). The inverse property of multiplication states that the product of a number (other than zero) and its reciprocal equals one. Reciprocal numbers have numerators and denominators that are inverted (ex. $\frac{2}{5}$ and $\frac{5}{2}$). Inverse properties are useful for canceling quantities to find missing values (see algebra content). For example, $a + 7 = 12$ is solved by adding the inverse of 7(-7) to both sides in order to isolate a.

The distributive property states that multiplying a sum (or difference) by a number produces the same result as multiplying each value in the sum (or difference) by the number and adding (or subtracting) the products. Consider the following scenario: You are buying three tickets for a baseball game. Each ticket costs $18. You are also charged a fee of $2 per ticket for purchasing the tickets online. The cost is calculated: $3 \times 18 + 3 \times 2$. Using the distributive property, the cost can also be calculated $3(18 + 2)$.

Factors and Multiples

The factors of a number are all integers that can be multiplied by another integer to produce the given number. For example, 2 is multiplied by 3 to produce 6. Therefore, 2 and 3 are both factors of 6. Similarly, $1 \times 6 = 6$ and $2 \times 3 = 6$, so one, 2, 3, and 6 are all factors of 6. Another way to explain a factor is to say that a given number divides evenly by each of its factors to produce an integer. For example, 6 does not divide evenly by 5. Therefore, 5 is not a factor of 6.

Multiples of a given number are found by taking that number and multiplying it by any other whole number. For example, 3 is a factor of 6, 9, and 12. Therefore, 6, 9, and 12 are multiples of 3. The multiples of any number are an infinite list. For example, the multiples of 5 are 5, 10, 15, 20, and so on. This list continues without end. A list of multiples is used in finding the least common multiple, or LCM, for fractions when a common denominator is needed. The denominators are written down and their multiples listed until a common number is found in both lists. This common number is the LCM.

Prime factorization breaks down each factor of a whole number until only prime numbers remain. All composite numbers can be factored into prime numbers. For example, the prime factors of 12 are 2, 2, and 3 ($2 \times 2 \times 3 = 12$). To produce the prime factors of a number, the number is factored and any composite numbers are continuously factored until the result is the product of prime factors only. A factor tree, such as the one below, is helpful when exploring this concept.

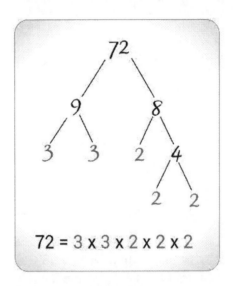

Roots and Square Roots

An *exponent* is written as a^b. In this expression, a is called the *base* and b is called the *exponent*. It is properly stated that a is raised to the n-th power. Therefore, in the expression 2^3, the exponent is 3, while the base is 2. Such an expression is called an *exponential expression*. Note that when the exponent is 2, it is called *squaring* the base, and when it is 3, it is called *cubing* the base.

When the exponent is a positive integer, this indicates the base is multiplied by itself the number of times written in the exponent. So, in the expression 2^3, multiply 2 by itself with 3 copies of 2: $2^3 = 2 \cdot 2 \cdot 2 = 8$. One thing to notice is that, for positive integers n and m, $a^n a^m = a^{n+m}$ is a rule. In order to make this rule be true for an integer of 0, $a^0 = 1$, so that $a^n a^0 = a^{n+0} = a^n$. And, in order to make this rule be true for negative exponents, $a^{-n} = \frac{1}{a^n}$.

Another rule for simplifying expressions with exponents is shown by the following equation: $(a^m)^n = a^{mn}$. This is true for fractional exponents as well. So, for a positive integer, define $a^{\frac{1}{n}}$ to be the number that, when raised to the n-th power, provides a. In other words, $(a^{\frac{1}{n}})^n = a$ is the desired equation. It should be noted that $a^{\frac{1}{n}}$ is the n-th root of a. This also can be written as $a^{\frac{1}{n}} = \sqrt[n]{a}$. The symbol on the right-hand side of this equation is called a *radical*. If the root is left out, assume that the 2nd root should be taken, also called the *square* root: $a^{\frac{1}{2}} = \sqrt[2]{a} = \sqrt{a}$. Additionally, $\sqrt[3]{a}$ is also called the *cube* root.

Note that when multiple roots exist, $a^{\frac{1}{n}}$ is defined to be the *positive* root. So, $4^{\frac{1}{2}} = 2$. Also note that negative numbers do not have even roots in the real numbers.

This also enables finding exponents for any rational number: $a^{\frac{m}{n}} = (a^{\frac{1}{n}})^m = (a^m)^{\frac{1}{n}}$. In fact, the exponent can be any real number. In general, the following rules for exponents should be used for any numbers $a, b, m,$ and n.

- $a^1 = a$.
- $1^a = 1$.
- $a^0 = 1$.
- $a^m a^n = a^{m+n}$.
- $\frac{a^m}{a^n} = a^{m-n}$
- $(a^m)^n = a^{m \times n}$.
- $(ab)^m = a^m b^m$.
- $\left(\frac{a}{b}\right)^m = \frac{a^m}{b^m}$.

As an example of applying these rules, consider the problem of simplifying the expression $(3x^2 y)^3 (2xy^4)$. Start by simplifying the left term using the sixth rule listed. Applying this rule yields the following expression: $27x^6 y^3 (2xy^4)$. The exponents can now be combined with base x and the exponents with base y. Multiply the coefficients to yield $54x^7 y^7$.

Polynomial Algebra
An expression of the form ax^n, where n is a non-negative integer, is called a *monomial* because it contains one term. A sum of monomials is called a *polynomial*. For example, $-4x^3 + x$ is a polynomial, while $5x^7$ is a monomial. A function equal to a polynomial is called a *polynomial function*.

The monomials in a polynomial are also called the *terms* of the polynomial.

The constants that precede the variables are called *coefficients*.

The highest value of the exponent of x in a polynomial is called the *degree* of the polynomial. So, $-4x^3 + x$ has a degree of 3, while $-2x^5 + x^3 + 4x + 1$ has a degree of 5. When multiplying polynomials, the degree of the result will be the sum of the degrees of the two polynomials being multiplied.

To add polynomials, add the coefficients of like powers of x. For example:

$$(-2x^5 + x^3 + 4x + 1) + (-4x^3 + x) = -2x^5 + (1-4)x^3 + (4+1)x + 1 = -2x^5 - 3x^3 + 5x + 1$$

Likewise, subtraction of polynomials is performed by subtracting coefficients of like powers of x. So, $(-2x^5 + x^3 + 4x + 1) - (-4x^3 + x) = -2x^5 + (1+4)x^3 + (4-1)x + 1 = -2x^5 + 5x^3 + 3x + 1$.

To multiply two polynomials, multiply each term of the first polynomial by each term of the second polynomial and add the results. For example:

$$(4x^2 + x)(-x^3 + x) = 4x^2(-x^3) + 4x^2(x) + x(-x^3) + x(x) = -4x^5 + 4x^3 - x^4 + x^2$$

In the case where each polynomial has two terms, like in this example, some students find it helpful to remember this as multiplying the First terms, then the Outer terms, then the Inner terms, and finally the Last terms, with the mnemonic FOIL. For longer polynomials, the multiplication process is the same, but there will be, of course, more terms, and there is no common mnemonic to remember each combination.

The process of *factoring* a polynomial means to write the polynomial as a product of other (generally simpler) polynomials. Here is an example: $x^2 - 4x + 3 = (x-1)(x-3)$. If a certain monomial divides every term of the polynomial, factor it out of each term, for example:

$$4x^3 + 16x^2 = 4x^2(x + 4).$$

$$x^2 + 2xy + y^2 = (x+y)^2 \text{ or } x^2 - 2xy + y^2 = (x-y)^2$$

$$x^2 - y^2 = (x+y)(x-y)$$

$$x^3 + y^3 = (x+y)(x^2 - xy + y^2)$$

$$x^3 - y^3 = (x-y)(x^2 + xy + y^2)$$

$$x^3 + 3x^2y + 3xy^2 + y^3 = (x+y)^3 \text{ and } x^3 - 3x^2y + 3xy^2 - y^3 = (x-y)^3$$

It sometimes can be necessary to rewrite the polynomial in some clever way before applying the above rules. Consider the problem of factoring $x^4 - 1$. This does not immediately look like any of the cases for which there are rules. However, it's possible to think of this polynomial as $x^4 - 1 = (x^2)^2 - (1^2)^2$, and now apply the third rule in the above list to simplify this:

$$(x^2)^2 - (1^2)^2 = (x^2 + 1^2)(x^2 - 1^2) = (x^2 + 1)(x^2 - 1)$$

Rational Expressions
A fraction, or ratio, wherein each part is a polynomial, defines *rational expressions*. Some examples include $\frac{2x+6}{x}$, $\frac{1}{x^2-4x+8}$, and $\frac{z^2}{x+5}$. Exponents on the variables are restricted to whole numbers, which means roots and negative exponents are not included in rational expressions.

Rational expressions can be transformed by factoring. For example, the expression $\frac{x^2-5x+6}{(x-3)}$ can be rewritten by factoring the numerator to obtain $\frac{(x-3)(x-2)}{(x-3)}$. Therefore, the common binomial $(x-3)$ can cancel so that the simplified expression is $\frac{(x-2)}{1} = (x-2)$.

Additionally, other rational expressions can be rewritten to take on different forms. Some may be factorable in themselves, while others can be transformed through arithmetic operations. Rational expressions are closed under addition, subtraction, multiplication, and division by a nonzero expression. *Closed* means that if any one of these operations is performed on a rational expression, the result will still be a rational expression. The set of all real numbers is another example of a set closed under all four operations.

Adding and subtracting rational expressions is based on the same concepts as adding and subtracting simple fractions. For both concepts, the denominators must be the same for the operation to take place. For example, here are two rational expressions:

$$\frac{x^3 - 4}{(x - 3)} + \frac{x + 8}{(x - 3)}$$

Since the denominators are both $(x - 3)$, the numerators can be combined by collecting like terms to form:

$$\frac{x^3 + x + 4}{(x - 3)}$$

If the denominators are different, they need to be made common (the same) by using the Least Common Denominator (LCD). Each denominator needs to be factored, and the LCD contains each factor that appears in any one denominator the greatest number of times it appears in any denominator. The original expressions need to be multiplied times a form of 1, which will turn each denominator into the LCD. This process is like adding fractions with unlike denominators. It is also important when working with rational expressions to define what value of the variable makes the denominator zero. For this particular value, the expression is undefined.

Multiplication of rational expressions is performed like multiplication of fractions. The numerators are multiplied; then, the denominators are multiplied. The final fraction is then simplified. The expressions are simplified by factoring and cancelling out common terms. In the following example, the numerator of the second expression can be factored first to simplify the expression before multiplying:

$$\frac{x^2}{(x - 4)} * \frac{x^2 - x - 12}{2}$$

$$\frac{x^2}{(x - 4)} * \frac{(x - 4)(x + 3)}{2}$$

The $(x - 4)$ on the top and bottom cancel out:

$$\frac{x^2}{1} * \frac{(x + 3)}{2}$$

Then multiplication is performed, resulting i:

$$\frac{x^3 + 3x^2}{2}$$

Dividing rational expressions is similar to the division of fractions, where division turns into multiplying by a reciprocal. So the following expression can be rewritten as a multiplication problem:

$$\frac{x^2 - 3x + 7}{x - 4} \div \frac{x^2 - 5x + 3}{x - 4}$$

$$\frac{x^2 - 3x + 7}{x - 4} * \frac{x - 4}{x^2 - 5x + 3}$$

The $x - 4$ cancels out, leaving:

$$\frac{x^2 - 3x + 7}{x^2 - 5x + 3}$$

The final answers should always be completely simplified. If a function is composed of a rational expression, the zeros of the graph can be found from setting the polynomial in the numerator as equal to zero and solving. The values that make the denominator equal to zero will either exist on the graph as a hole or a vertical asymptote.

Equations and Inequalities
An equation contains two sides separated by an equal sign. Equations can be solved to determine the value(s) of the variable for which the statement is true.

Assume the sum of a number and 5 is equal to 10 times the number. To find this unknown number, a simple equation can be written to represent the problem. Key words such as *sum*, *equal*, and *times* are used to form the following equation with one variable: $n + 5 = 10n$. When solving for n, opposite operations are used. First, n is subtracted from $10n$ across the equals sign, resulting in $5 = 9n$. Then, 9 is divided on both sides, leaving $n = \frac{5}{9}$. This solution can be graphed on the number line with a dot as shown below:

If the problem were changed to say, "The sum of a number and 5 is greater than 10 times the number," then an inequality would be used instead of an equation. Using key words again, *greater than* is represented by the symbol >. The inequality $n + 5 > 10n$ can be solved using the same techniques, resulting in $n < \frac{5}{9}$. The only time solving an inequality differs from solving an equation is when a negative number is either multiplied times or divided by each side of the inequality. The sign must be switched in this case. For this example, the graph of the solution changes to the following graph because the solution represents all real numbers less than $\frac{5}{9}$. Not included in this solution is $\frac{5}{9}$ because it is a *less than* symbol, not *equal to*.

Equations and inequalities in two variables represent a relationship. Jim owns a car wash and charges $40 per car. The rent for the facility is $350 per month. An equation can be written to relate the number of cars Jim cleans to the money he makes per month. Let x represent the number of cars and y represent the profit Jim makes each month from the car wash. The equation $y = 40x - 350$ can be used to show Jim's profit or loss. Since this equation has two variables, the coordinate plane can be used to show the relationship and predict profit or loss for Jim. The following graph shows that Jim must wash at least nine cars to pay the rent, where $x = 9$.

Anything nine cars and above will yield a profit as shown by the value on the y-axis.

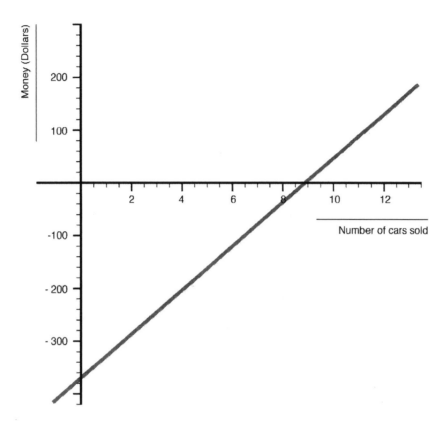

With a single equation in two variables, the solutions are limited only by the situation the equation represents. When two equations or inequalities are used, more constraints are added. For example, in a system of linear equations, there is often—although not always—only one answer. The point of intersection of two lines is the solution. For a system of inequalities, there are infinitely many answers.

The intersection of two solution sets gives the solution set of the system of inequalities. In the following graph, the darker shaded region with the swirls where the shading for the two inequalities overlap. Any set of x and y found in that region satisfies both inequalities. The line with the positive slope is solid, meaning the values on that line are included in the solution.

The line with the negative slope is dotted, so the coordinates on that line are not included.

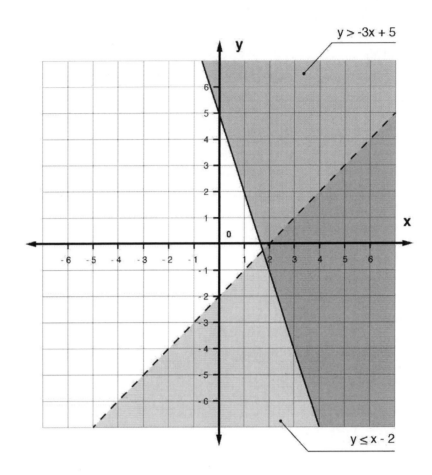

Formulas with two variables are equations used to represent a specific relationship. For example, the formula $d = rt$ represents the relationship between distance, rate, and time. If Bob travels at a rate of 35 miles per hour on his road trip from Westminster to Seneca, the formula $d = 35t$ can be used to represent his distance traveled in a specific length of time. Formulas can also be used to show different roles of the variables, transformed without any given numbers. Solving for r, the formula becomes $\frac{d}{t} = r$. The t is moved over by division so that *rate* is a function of distance and time.

Solving Equations
Solving equations in one variable is the process of isolating that variable on one side of the equation. For example, in $3x - 7 = 20$, the variable x needs to be isolated. Using opposite operations, the -7 is moved to the right side of the equation by adding seven to both sides:

$$3x - 7 + 7 = 20 + 7$$

$$3x = 27$$

Dividing by three on each side, $\frac{3x}{3} = \frac{27}{3}$, results in isolation of the variable. It is important to note that if an operation is performed on one side of the equals sign, it has to be performed on the other side to maintain equality. The solution is found to be $x = 9$. This solution can be checked for accuracy by plugging $x=7$ in the original equation. After simplifying the equation, $20 = 20$ is found, which is a true statement.

When solving radical and rational equations, extraneous solutions must be accounted for when finding the answers. For example, the equation $\frac{x}{x-5} = \frac{3x}{x+3}$ has two values that create a 0 denominator: $x \neq 5, -3$. When solving for x, these values must be considered because they cannot be solutions. In the given equation, solving for x can be done using cross-multiplication, yielding the equation:

$$x(x + 3) = 3x(x - 5)$$

Distributing results in the quadratic equation yields $x^2 + 3x = 3x^2 - 15x$; therefore, all terms must be moved to one side of the equals sign. This results in $2x^2 - 18x = 0$, which in factored form is $2x(x - 9) = 0$. Setting each factor equal to zero, the apparent solutions are $x = 0$ and $x = 9$. These two solutions are neither 5 nor -3, so they are viable solutions. Neither 0 nor 9 create a 0 denominator in the original equation.

A similar process exists when solving radical equations. One must check to make sure the solutions are defined in the original equations. Solving an equation containing a square root involves isolating the root and then squaring both sides of the equals sign. Solving a cube root equation involves isolating the radical and then cubing both sides. In either case, the variable can then be solved for because there are no longer radicals in the equation.

Equations with one variable can be solved using the addition principle and multiplication principle. If $a = b$, then $a + c = b + c$, and $ac = bc$. Given the equation $2x - 3 = 5x + 7$, the first step is to combine the variable terms and the constant terms. Using the principles, expressions can be added and subtracted onto and off both sides of the equals sign, so the equation turns into $-10 = 3x$. Dividing by 3 on both sides through the multiplication principle with $c = \frac{1}{3}$ results in the final answer of $x = \frac{-10}{3}$.

Some equations have a higher degree and are not solved by simply using opposite operations. When an equation has a degree of 2, completing the square is an option. For example, the quadratic equation $x^2 - 6x + 2 = 0$ can be rewritten by completing the square. A *quadratic equation* is an equation in the form $ax^2 + bx + c = 0$. The goal of completing the square is to get the equation into the form $(x - p)^2 = q$. Using the example, the constant term 2 first needs to be moved over to the opposite side by subtracting. Then, the square can be completed by adding 9 to both sides, which is the square of half of the coefficient of the middle term $-6x$. The current equation is $x^2 - 6x + 9 = 7$. The left side can be factored into a square of a binomial, resulting in $(x - 3)^2 = 7$. To solve for x, the square root of both sides should be taken, resulting in:

$$(x - 3) = \pm\sqrt{7}$$

$$x = 3 \pm \sqrt{7}$$

Other ways of solving quadratic equations include graphing, factoring, and using the quadratic formula. The equation $y = x^2 - 4x + 3$ can be graphed on the coordinate plane, and the solutions can be observed where it crosses the x-axis. The graph will be a parabola that opens up with two solutions at 1 and 3.

The equation can also be factored to find the solutions. The original equation, $y = x^2 - 4x + 3$ can be factored into $y = (x - 1)(x - 3)$. Setting this equal to zero, the x-values are found to be 1 and 3, just as on the graph. Solving by factoring and graphing are not always possible. The quadratic formula is a method of solving quadratic equations that always results in exact solutions.

The formula is:

$$x = \frac{-b \pm \sqrt{b^2 - 4ac}}{2a}$$

where $a, b,$ and c are the coefficients in the original equation in standard form $y = ax^2 + bx + c$. For this example,

$$x = \frac{4 \pm \sqrt{(-4)^2 - 4(1)(3)}}{2(1)} = \frac{4 \pm \sqrt{16 - 12}}{2} = \frac{4 \pm 2}{2} = 1, 3$$

The expression underneath the radical is called the *discriminant*. Without working out the entire formula, the value of the discriminant can reveal the nature of the solutions. If the value of the discriminant $b^2 - 4ac$ is positive, then there will be two real solutions. If the value is zero, there will be one real solution. If the value is negative, the two solutions will be imaginary or complex. If the solutions are complex, it means that the parabola never touches the x-axis. An example of a complex solution can be found by solving the following quadratic: $y = x^2 - 4x + 8$. By using the quadratic formula, the solutions are found to be:

$$x = \frac{4 \pm \sqrt{(-4)^2 - 4(1)(8)}}{2(1)} = \frac{4 \pm \sqrt{16 - 32}}{2} = \frac{4 \pm \sqrt{-16}}{2} = 2 \pm 2i$$

The solutions both have a real part, 2, and an imaginary part, $2i$.

Systems of Equations

A *system of equations* is a group of equations that have the same variables or unknowns. These equations can be linear, but they are not always so. Finding a solution to a system of equations means finding the values of the variables that satisfy each equation. For a linear system of two equations and two variables, there could be a single solution, no solution, or infinitely many solutions.

A single solution occurs when there is one value for x and y that satisfies the system. This would be shown on the graph where the lines cross at exactly one point. When there is no solution, the lines are parallel and do not ever cross. With infinitely many solutions, the equations may look different, but they are the same line. One equation will be a multiple of the other, and on the graph, they lie on top of each other.

The process of elimination can be used to solve a system of equations. Using *elimination* means the equations are added together, and one variable cancels out. For example, the following equations make up a system:

$$x + 3y = 10 \text{ and } 2x - 5y = 9$$

Immediately adding these equations does not eliminate a variable, but it is possible to change the first equation by multiplying the whole equation by -2. This changes the first equation to

$$-2x - 6y = -20$$

The equations can be then added to obtain $-11y = -11$. Solving for y yields $y = 1$. To find the rest of the solution, 1 can be substituted in for y in either original equation to find the value of $x = 7$. The solution to the system is (7, 1) because it makes both equations true, and it is the point in which the

lines intersect. If the system is *dependent*—having infinitely many solutions—then both variables will cancel out when the elimination method is used, resulting in an equation that is true for many values of x and y. Since the system is dependent, both equations can be simplified to the same equation or line.

A system can also be solved using *substitution*. This involves solving one equation for a variable and then plugging that solved equation into the other equation in the system. This equation can be solved for one variable, which can then be plugged in to either original equation and solved for the other variable. For example, $x - y = -2$ and $3x + 2y = 9$ can be solved using substitution. The first equation can be solved for x, where $x = -2 + y$. Then it can be plugged into the other equation:

$$3(-2 + y) + 2y = 9$$

Solving for y yields:

$$-6 + 3y + 2y = 9$$

That shows that $y = 3$. If $y = 3$, then $x = 1$.

This solution can be checked by plugging in these values for the variables in each equation to see if it makes a true statement.

Finally, a solution to a system of equations can be found graphically. The solution to a linear system is the point or points where the lines cross. The values of x and y represent the coordinates (x, y) where the lines intersect. Using the same system of equation as above, they can be solved for y to put them in slope-intercept form, $y = mx + b$. These equations become $y = x + 4$ and $y = -\frac{3}{2}x + 4.5$. The slope is the coefficient of x, and the y-intercept is the constant value. This system with the solution is shown below:

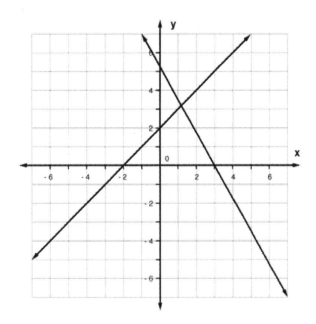

A system of equations may also be made up of a linear and a quadratic equation. These systems may have one solution, two solutions, or no solutions. The graph of these systems involves one straight line and one parabola. Algebraically, these systems can be solved by solving the linear equation for one variable and plugging that answer in to the quadratic equation. If possible, the equation can then be solved to find part of the answer. The graphing method is commonly used for these types of systems. On a graph, these two lines can be found to intersect at one point, at two points across the parabola, or at no points.

Equations and Graphing

A function is called *linear* if it can take the form of the equation $f(x) = ax + b$, or $y = ax + b$, for any two numbers a and b. A linear equation forms a straight line when graphed on the coordinate plane. An example of a linear function is shown below on the graph.

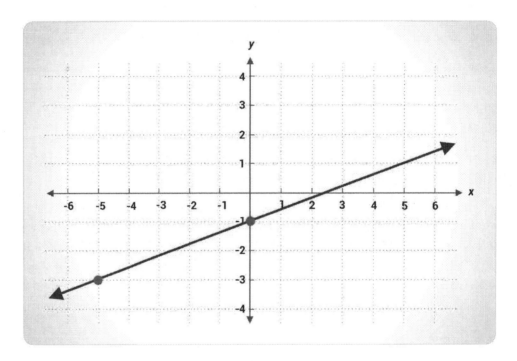

This is a graph of the following function: $y = \frac{2}{5}x - 1$. A table of values that satisfies this function is shown below.

x	y
-5	-3
0	-1
5	1
10	3

These points can be found on the graph using the form (x,y).

To graph relations and functions, the Cartesian plane is used. This means to think of the plane as being given a grid of squares, with one direction being the x-axis and the other direction the y-axis. Generally, the independent variable is placed along the horizontal axis, and the dependent variable is placed along the vertical axis. Any point on the plane can be specified by saying how far to go along the x-axis and how far along the y-axis with a pair of numbers (x, y). Specific values for these pairs can be given names such as $C = (-1, 3)$. Negative values mean to move left or down; positive values mean to move right or up. The point where the axes cross one another is called the *origin*. The origin has coordinates $(0, 0)$ and is usually called O when given a specific label. An illustration of the Cartesian plane, along with graphs of $(2, 1)$ and $(-1, -1)$, are below.

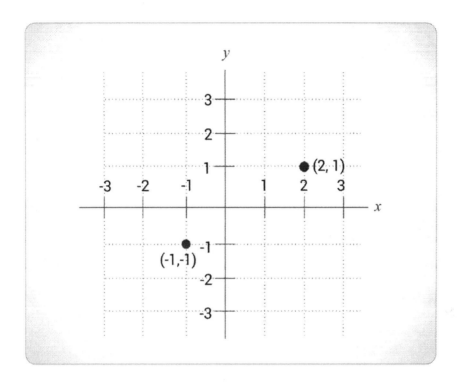

Relations also can be graphed by marking each point whose coordinates satisfy the relation. If the relation is a function, then there is only one value of y for any given value of x. This leads to the *vertical line test*: if a relation is graphed, then the relation is a function if every vertical line touches the graph at either zero or one point. Conversely, when graphing a function, then every vertical line will touch the graph at no points or just one point.

When graphing a linear function, note that the ratio of the change of the y coordinate to the change in the x coordinate is constant between any two points on the resulting line, no matter which two points are chosen. In other words, in a pair of points on a line, (x_1, y_1) and (x_2, y_2), with $x_1 \neq x_2$ so that the two points are distinct, then the ratio $\frac{y_2 - y_1}{x_2 - x_1}$ will be the same, regardless of which particular pair of points are chosen. This ratio, $\frac{y_2 - y_1}{x_2 - x_1}$, is called the *slope* of the line and is frequently denoted with the letter m. If slope m is positive, then the line goes upward when moving to the right, while if slope m is negative, then the line goes downward when moving to the right. If the slope is 0, then the line is called *horizontal*, and the y coordinate is constant along the entire line. In lines where the x coordinate is constant along the entire line, y is not actually a function of x. For such lines, the slope is not defined. These lines are called *vertical* lines.

Linear functions may take forms other than $y = ax + b$. The most common forms of linear equations are explained below:

1. Standard Form: $Ax + By = C$, in which the slope is given by $m = \frac{-A}{B}$, and the y-intercept is given by $\frac{C}{B}$.

2. Slope-Intercept Form: $y = mx + b$, where the slope is m and the y intercept is b.

3. Point-Slope Form: $y - y_1 = m(x - x_1)$, where the slope is m and (x_1, y_1) is any point on the chosen line.

4. Two-Point Form: $\frac{y-y_1}{x-x_1} = \frac{y_2-y_1}{x_2-x_1}$, where (x_1, y_1) and (x_2, y_2) are any two distinct points on the chosen line. Note that the slope is given by $m = \frac{y_2-y_1}{x_2-x_1}$.

5. Intercept Form: $\frac{x}{x_1} + \frac{y}{y_1} = 1$, in which x_1 is the x-intercept and y_1 is the y-intercept.

These five ways to write linear equations are all useful in different circumstances. Depending on the given information, it may be easier to write one of the forms over another.

If $y = mx$, y is directly proportional to x. In this case, changing x by a factor changes y by that same factor. If $y = \frac{m}{x}$, y is inversely proportional to x. For example, if x is increased by a factor of 3, then y will be decreased by the same factor, 3.

The *midpoint* between two points, (x_1, y_1) and (x_2, y_2), is given by taking the average of the x coordinates and the average of the y coordinates:

$$\left(\frac{x_1 + x_2}{2}, \frac{y_1 + y_2}{2}\right)$$

The *distance* between two points, (x_1, y_1) and (x_2, y_2), is given by the *Pythagorean formula*, $\sqrt{(x_2 - x_1)^2 + (y_2 - y_1)^2}$.

To find the perpendicular distance between a line $Ax + By = C$ and a point (x_1, y_1) not on the line, we need to use the formula

$$\frac{|Ax_1 + By_1 + C|}{\sqrt{A^2 + B^2}}$$

Functions
A *function* is defined as a relationship between inputs and outputs where there is only one output value for a given input. The input is called the *independent variable*. If the variable is set equal to the output, as in $y = f(x)$, then this is called the *dependent variable*. To indicate the dependent value a function, y, gives for a specific independent variable, x, the notation y = $f(x)$ is used.

As an example, the following function is in function notation: $f(x) = 3x - 4$. The $f(x)$ represents the output value for an input of x. If $x = 2$, the equation becomes:

$$f(2) = 3(2) - 4 = 6 - 4 = 2$$

The input of 2 yields an output of 2, forming the ordered pair $(2, 2)$. The following set of ordered pairs corresponds to the given function: $(2, 2), (0, -4), (-2, -10)$. The set of all possible inputs of a function is its *domain*, and all possible outputs is called the *range*. By definition, each member of the domain is paired with only one member of the range.

Functions can also be defined recursively. In this form, they are not defined explicitly in terms of variables. Instead, they are defined using previously-evaluated function outputs, starting with either $f(0)$ or $f(1)$. An example of a recursively-defined function is:

$$f(1) = 2, f(n) = 2f(n-1) + 2n, n > 1$$

The domain of this function is the set of all integers.

The domain and range of a function can be found visually by its plot on the coordinate plane. In the function $f(x) = x^2 - 3$, for example, the domain is all real numbers because the parabola stretches as far left and as far right as it can go, with no restrictions. This means that any input value from the real number system will yield an answer in the real number system. For the range, the inequality $y \geq -3$ would be used to describe the possible output values because the parabola has a minimum at $y = -3$. This means there will not be any real output values less than -3 because -3 is the lowest value it reaches on the y-axis.

These same answers for domain and range can be found by observing a table. The table below shows that from input values $x = -1$ to $x = 1$, the output results in a minimum of -3. On each side of $x = 0$, the numbers increase, showing that the range is all real numbers greater than or equal to -3.

x (domain/input)	y (range/output)
-2	1
-1	-2
0	-3
-1	-2
2	1

Different types of functions behave in different ways. The quadratic function described above can be described as decreasing from left to right until the input value of zero, then increasing after that. A function is defined to be increasing over a subset of its domain if for all $x_1 \geq x_2$ in that interval, $f(x_1) \geq f(x_2)$. Also, a function is decreasing over an interval if for all $x_1 \geq x_2$ in that interval, $f(x_1) \leq f(x_2)$. A point in which a function changes from increasing to decreasing can also be labeled as the *maximum value* of a function if it is the largest point the graph reaches on the y-axis. A point in which a function changes from decreasing to increasing can be labeled as the minimum value of a function if it is the smallest point the graph reaches on the y-axis. Maximum values are also known as *extreme values*. The graph of a continuous function does not have any breaks or jumps in the graph. This description is not true of all functions. A radical function, for example, $f(x) = \sqrt{x}$, has a restriction for the domain and range because there are no real negative inputs or outputs for this function. The domain can be stated as $x \geq 0$, and the range is $y \geq 0$.

A piecewise-defined function also has a different appearance on the graph. In the following function, there are three equations defined over different intervals. It is a function because there is only one y-value for each x-value, passing the Vertical Line Test. The domain is all real numbers less than or equal to 6. The range is all real numbers greater than 0. From left to right, the graph decreases to 0, then increases to almost 4, and then jumps to 6.

From input values greater than 2, the input decreases just below 8 to 4, and then stops.

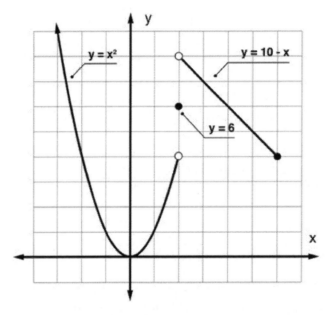

Logarithmic and exponential functions also have different behavior than other functions. These two types of functions are inverses of each other. The *inverse* of a function can be found by switching the place of x and y, and solving for y. When this is done for the exponential equation, $y = 2^x$, the function $y = \log_2 x$ is found. The general form of a *logarithmic function* is $y = \log_b x$, which says b raised to the y power equals x.

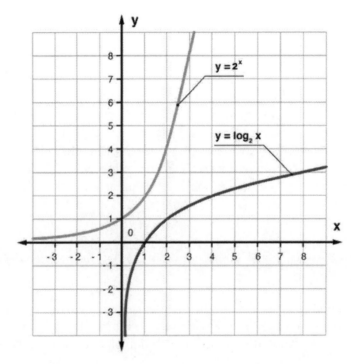

The thick black line on the graph above represents the logarithmic function $y = \log_2 x$. This curve passes through the point $(1, 0)$, just as all log functions do, because any value $b^0 = 1$. The graph of this logarithmic function starts very close to zero, but does not touch the y-axis. The output value will never be zero by the definition of logarithms. The thinner gray line seen above represents the exponential function $y = 2^x$. The behavior of this function is opposite the logarithmic function because the graph of an inverse function is the graph of the original function flipped over the line $y = x$. The curve passes through the point $(0, 1)$ because any number raised to the zero power is one. This curve also gets very close to the x-axis but never touches it because an exponential expression never has an output of zero. The x-axis on this graph is called a horizontal asymptote. An *asymptote* is a line that represents a boundary for a function. It shows a value that the function will get close to, but never reach.

Functions can also be described as being even, odd, or neither. If $f(-x) = f(x)$, the function is even. For example, the function $f(x) = x^2 - 2$ is even. Plugging in $x = 2$ yields an output of $y = 2$. After changing the input to $x = -2$, the output is still $y = 2$. The output is the same for opposite inputs. Another way to observe an even function is by the symmetry of the graph. If the graph is symmetrical about the axis, then the function is even. If the graph is symmetric about the origin, then the function is odd. Algebraically, if $f(-x) = -f(x)$, the function is odd.

Finally, a function can be described as *periodic* if it repeats itself in regular intervals. Common periodic functions are trigonometric functions. For example, $y = \sin x$ is a periodic function with period 2π because it repeats itself every 2π units along the x-axis.

Building Functions

Functions can be built out of the context of a situation. For example, the relationship between the money paid for a gym membership and the months that someone has been a member can be described through a function. If the one-time membership fee is $40 and the monthly fee is $30, then the function can be written $f(x) = 30x + 40$. The x-value represents the number of months the person has been part of the gym, while the output is the total money paid for the membership. The table below shows this relationship. It is a representation of the function because the initial cost is $40 and the cost increases each month by $30.

x (months)	y (money paid to gym)
0	40
1	70
2	100
3	130

Functions can also be built from existing functions. For example, a given function $f(x)$ can be transformed by adding a constant, multiplying by a constant, or changing the input value by a constant. The new function $g(x) = f(x) + k$ represents a vertical shift of the original function. In $f(x) = 3x - 2$, a vertical shift 4 units up would be:

$$g(x) = 3x - 2 + 4 = 3x + 2$$

Multiplying the function times a constant k represents a vertical stretch, based on whether the constant is greater than or less than 1. The following function represents a stretch:

$$g(x) = kf(x) = 4(3x - 2) = 12x - 8$$

35

Changing the input x by a constant forms the function:

$$g(x) = f(x + k) = 3(x + 4) - 2 = 3x + 12 - 2 = 3x + 10$$

and this represents a horizontal shift to the left 4 units. If $(x - 4)$ was plugged into the function, it would represent a vertical shift.

A composition function can also be formed by plugging one function into another. In function notation, this is written:

$$(f \circ g)(x) = f(g(x))$$

For two functions $f(x) = x^2$ and $g(x) = x - 3$, the composition function becomes:

$$f(g(x)) = (x - 3)^2 = x^2 - 6x + 9$$

The composition of functions can also be used to verify if two functions are inverses of each other. Given the two functions $f(x) = 2x + 5$ and $g(x) = \frac{x-5}{2}$, the composition function can be found $(f \circ g)(x)$. Solving this equation yields:

$$f(g(x)) = 2\left(\frac{x - 5}{2}\right) + 5 = x - 5 + 5 = x$$

It also is true that $g(f(x)) = x$. Since the composition of these two functions gives a simplified answer of x, this verifies that $f(x)$ and $g(x)$ are inverse functions. The domain of $f(g(x))$ is the set of all x-values in the domain of $g(x)$ such that $g(x)$ is in the domain of $f(x)$. Basically, both $f(g(x))$ and $g(x)$ have to be defined.

To build an inverse of a function, $f(x)$ needs to be replaced with y, and the x and y values need to be switched. Then, the equation can be solved for y. For example, given the equation $y = e^{2x}$, the inverse can be found by rewriting the equation $x = e^{2y}$. The natural logarithm of both sides is taken down, and the exponent is brought down to form the equation:

$$\ln(x) = \ln(e)\, 2y$$

$\ln(e)$=1, which yields the equation $\ln(x) = 2y$. Dividing both sides by 2 yields the inverse equation

$$\frac{\ln(x)}{2} = y = f^{-1}(x)$$

The domain of an inverse function is the range of the original function, and the range of an inverse function is the domain of the original function. Therefore, an ordered pair (x, y) on either a graph or a table corresponding to $f(x)$ means that the ordered pair (y, x) exists on the graph of $f^{-1}(x)$. Basically, if $f(x) = y$, then $f^{-1}(y) = x$. For a function have an inverse, it must be one-to-one. That means it must pass the *Horizontal Line Test*, and if any horizontal line passes through the graph of the function twice, a function is not one-to-one. The domain of a function that is not one-to-one can be restricted to an interval in which the function is one-to-one, to be able to define an inverse function.

Functions can also be formed from combinations of existing functions.

Given $f(x)$ and $g(x)$, the following can be built:

$$f + g$$

$$f - g$$

$$fg$$

$$\frac{f}{g}$$

The domains of $f + g$, $f - g$, and fg are the intersection of the domains of f and g. The domain of $\frac{f}{g}$ is the same set, excluding those values that make $g(x) = 0$.

For example, if:

$$f(x) = 2x + 3$$

$$g(x) = x + 1$$

then

$$\frac{f}{g} = \frac{2x + 3}{x + 1}$$

Its domain is all real numbers except -1.

Common Functions

Three common functions used to model different relationships between quantities are linear, quadratic, and exponential functions. Linear functions are the simplest of the three, and the independent variable x has an exponent of 1. Written in the most common form, $y = mx + b$, the coefficient of x tells how fast the function grows at a constant rate, and the b-value tells the starting point. A quadratic function has an exponent of 2 on the independent variable x. Standard form for this type of function is $y = ax^2 + bx + c$, and the graph is a parabola. These type functions grow at a changing rate. An exponential function has an independent variable in the exponent $y = ab^x$. The graph of these types of functions is described as *growth* or *decay*, based on whether the base, b, is greater than or less than 1. These functions are different from quadratic functions because the base stays constant. A common base is base e.

The following three functions model a linear, quadratic, and exponential function respectively: $y = 2x$, $y = x^2$, and $y = 2^x$. Their graphs are shown below. The first graph, modeling the linear function, shows that the growth is constant over each interval. With a horizontal change of 1, the vertical change is 2. It models a constant positive growth. The second graph shows the quadratic function, which is a curve that is symmetric across the y-axis. The growth is not constant, but the change is mirrored over the axis. The last graph models the exponential function, where the horizontal change of 1 yields a vertical change that increases more and more. The exponential graph gets very close to the x-axis, but never touches it, meaning there is an asymptote there. The y-value can never be zero because the base of 2 can never be raised to an input value that yields an output of zero.

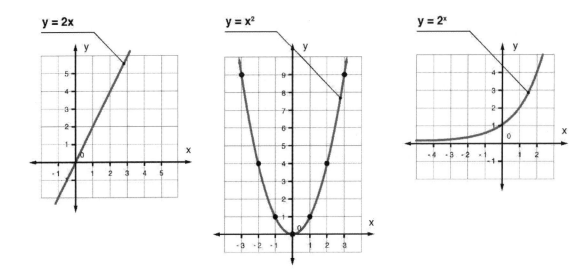

The three tables below show specific values for three types of functions. The third column in each table shows the change in the y-values for each interval. The first table shows a constant change of 2 for each equal interval, which matches the slope in the equation $y = 2x$. The second table shows an increasing change, but it also has a pattern. The increase is changing by 2 more each time, so the change is quadratic. The third table shows the change as factors of the base, 2. It shows a continuing pattern of factors of the base.

y = 2x		
x	y	$\triangle y$
1	2	
2	4	2
3	6	2
4	8	2
5	10	2

$y = x^2$		
x	y	$\triangle y$
1	1	
2	4	3
3	9	5
4	16	7
5	25	9

$y = 2^x$		
x	y	$\triangle y$
1	2	
2	4	2
3	8	4
4	16	8
5	32	16

Given a table of values, the type of function can be determined by observing the change in y over equal intervals. For example, the tables below model two functions. The changes in interval for the x-values is 1 for both tables. For the first table, the y-values increase by 5 for each interval. Since the change is constant, the situation can be described as a linear function. The equation would be $y = 5x + 3$. For the second table, the change for y is 5, 20, 100, and 500, respectively. The increases are multiples of 5, meaning the situation can be modeled by an exponential function. The equation $y = 5^x + 3$ models this situation.

x	y
0	3
1	8
2	13
3	18
4	23

x	y
0	3
1	8
2	28
3	128
4	628

Quadratic equations can be used to model real-world area problems. For example, a farmer may have a rectangular field that he needs to sow with seed. The field has length $x + 8$ and width $2x$. The formula for area should be used: $A = lw$. Therefore:

$$A = (x + 8) * 2x = 2x^2 + 16x$$

The possible values for the length and width can be shown in a table, with input x and output A. If the equation was graphed, the possible area values can be seen on the y-axis for given x-values.

Exponential growth and decay can be found in real-world situations. For example, if a piece of notebook paper is folded 25 times, the thickness of the paper can be found. To model this situation, a table can be used. The initial point is one-fold, which yields a thickness of 2 papers. For the second fold, the thickness is 4. Since the thickness doubles each time, the table below shows the thickness for the next few folds. Notice the thickness changes by the same factor each time. Since this change for a constant interval of folds is a factor of 2, the function is exponential. The equation for this is $y = 2^x$. For twenty-five folds, the thickness would be 33,554,432 papers.

x (folds)	y (paper thickness)
0	1
1	2
2	4
3	8
4	16
5	32

One exponential formula that is commonly used is the *interest formula*: $A = Pe^{rt}$. In this formula, interest is compounded continuously. A is the value of the investment after the time, t, in years. P is the initial amount of the investment, r is the interest rate, and e is the constant equal to approximately 2.718. Given an initial amount of $200 and a time of 3 years, if interest is compounded continuously at a rate of 6%, the total investment value can be found by plugging each value into the formula. The invested value at the end is $239.44. In more complex problems, the final investment may be given, and the rate may be the unknown. In this case, the formula becomes $239.44 = 200e^{r3}$. Solving for r requires isolating the exponential expression on one side by dividing by 200, yielding the equation

$1.20 = e^{r3}$. Taking the natural log of both sides results in $\ln(1.2) = r3$. Using a calculator to evaluate the logarithmic expression, $r = 0.06 = 6\%$.

When working with logarithms and exponential expressions, it is important to remember the relationship between the two. In general, the logarithmic form is $y = log_b x$ for an exponential form $b^y = x$. Logarithms and exponential functions are inverses of each other.

Patterns

Patterns within a sequence can come in 2 distinct forms: the items (shapes, numbers, etc.) either repeat in a constant order, or the items change from one step to another in some consistent way. The core is the smallest unit, or number of items, that repeats in a repeating pattern. For example, the pattern ○○▲○○▲○... has a core that is ○○▲. Knowing only the core, the pattern can be extended. Knowing the number of steps in the core allows the identification of an item in each step without drawing/writing the entire pattern out. For example, suppose the tenth item in the previous pattern must be determined. Because the core consists of three items (○○▲), the core repeats in multiples of 3. In other words, steps 3, 6, 9, 12, etc. will be ▲ completing the core with the core starting over on the next step. For the above example, the 9th step will be ▲ and the 10th will be ○.

The most common patterns in which each item changes from one step to the next are arithmetic and geometric sequences. An arithmetic sequence is one in which the items increase or decrease by a constant difference. In other words, the same thing is added or subtracted to each item or step to produce the next. To determine if a sequence is arithmetic, determine what must be added or subtracted to step one to produce step two. Then, check if the same thing is added/subtracted to step two to produce step three. The same thing must be added/subtracted to step three to produce step four, and so on. Consider the pattern 13, 10, 7, 4 . . . To get from step one (13) to step two (10) by adding or subtracting requires subtracting by 3. The next step is checking if subtracting 3 from step two (10) will produce step three (7), and subtracting 3 from step three (7) will produce step four (4). In this case, the pattern holds true. Therefore, this is an arithmetic sequence in which each step is produced by subtracting 3 from the previous step. To extend the sequence, 3 is subtracted from the last step to produce the next. The next three numbers in the sequence are 1, -2, -5.

A geometric sequence is one in which each step is produced by multiplying or dividing the previous step by the same number. To determine if a sequence is geometric, decide what step one must be multiplied or divided by to produce step two. Then check if multiplying or dividing step two by the same number produces step three, and so on. Consider the pattern 2, 8, 32, 128 . . . To get from step one (2) to step two (8) requires multiplication by 4. The next step determines if multiplying step two (8) by 4 produces step three (32), and multiplying step three (32) by 4 produces step four (128). In this case, the pattern holds true. Therefore, this is a geometric sequence in which each step is produced by multiplying the previous step by 4. To extend the sequence, the last step is multiplied by 4 and repeated. The next three numbers in the sequence are 512; 2,048; 8,192.

Although arithmetic and geometric sequences typically use numbers, these sequences can also be represented by shapes. For example, an arithmetic sequence could consist of shapes with three sides, four sides, and five sides (add one side to the previous step to produce the next). A geometric sequence could consist of eight blocks, four blocks, and two blocks (each step is produced by dividing the number of blocks in the previous step by 2).

An arithmetic or geometric sequence can be written as a formula and used to determine unknown steps without writing out the entire sequence. An arithmetic sequence progresses by a *common difference*. To determine the common difference, any step is subtracted by the step that precedes it. In the sequence 4, 9, 14, 19 . . . the common difference, or d, is 5. By expressing each step as a_1, a_2, a_3, etc., a formula can be written to represent the sequence. a_1 is the first step. To produce step two, step 1 (a_1) is added to the common difference (d): $a_2 = a_1 + d$. To produce step three, the common difference (d) is added twice to a_1: $a_3 = a_1 + 2d$. To produce step four, the common difference (d) is added three times to a_1: $a_4 = a_1 + 3d$. Following this pattern allows a general rule for arithmetic sequences to be written. For any term of the sequence (a_n), the first step (a_1) is added to the product of the common difference (d) and one less than the step of the term ($n - 1$): $a_n = a_1 + (n - 1)d$. Suppose the 8th term (a_8) is to be found in the previous sequence. By knowing the first step (a_1) is 4 and the common difference (d) is 5, the formula can be used: $a_n = a_1 + (n - 1)d \rightarrow a_8 = 4 + (7)5 \rightarrow a_8 = 39$.

In a geometric sequence, each step is produced by multiplying or dividing the previous step by the same number. The *common ratio*, or (r), can be determined by dividing any step by the previous step. In the sequence 1, 3, 9, 27 . . . the common ratio (r) is 3 ($\frac{3}{1} = 3$ or $\frac{9}{3} = 3$ or $\frac{27}{9} = 3$). Each successive step can be expressed as a product of the first step (a_1) and the common ratio (r) to some power. For example, $a_2 = a_1 \times r$; $a_3 = a_1 \times r \times r$ or $a_3 = a_1 \times r^2$; $a_4 = a_1 \times r \times r \times r$ or $a_4 = a\_1 \times r^3$. Following this pattern, a general rule for geometric sequences can be written. For any term of the sequence (a_n), the first step (a_1) is multiplied by the common ratio (r) raised to the power one less than the step of the term ($n - 1$): $a_n = a_1 \times r^{(n-1)}$. Suppose for the previous sequence, the 7th term (a_7) is to be found. Knowing the first step (a_1) is one, and the common ratio (r) is 3, the formula can be used: $a_n = a_1 \times r^{(n-1)} \rightarrow a_7 = (1) \times 3^6 \rightarrow a_7 = 729$.

Data Analysis, Probability, and Statistics

Statistics
The field of statistics describes relationships between quantities that are related, but not necessarily in a deterministic manner. For example, a graduating student's salary will often be higher when the student graduates with a higher GPA, but this is not always the case. Likewise, people who smoke tobacco are more likely to develop lung cancer, but, in fact, it is possible for non-smokers to develop the disease as well. *Statistics* describes these kinds of situations, where the likelihood of some outcome depends on the starting data.

Descriptive statistics involves analyzing a collection of data to describe its broad properties such average (or mean), what percent of the data falls within a given range, and other such properties. An example of this would be taking all of the test scores from a given class and calculating the average test score. *Inferential statistics* attempts to use data about a subset of some population to make inferences about the rest of the population. An example of this would be taking a collection of students who received tutoring and comparing their results to a collection of students who did not receive tutoring, then using that comparison to try to predict whether the tutoring program in question is beneficial.

To be sure that inferences have a high probability of being true for the whole population, the subset that is analyzed needs to resemble a miniature version of the population as closely as possible. For this reason, statisticians like to choose random samples from the population to study, rather than picking a specific group of people based on some similarity. For example, studying the incomes of people who live in Portland does not tell anything useful about the incomes of people who live in Tallahassee.

Measures of Central Tendency
Suppose that X is a set of data points ($x_1, x_2, x_3, \dots x_n$) and some description of the general properties of this data need to be found.

The first property that can be defined for this set of data is the *mean*. To find the mean, add up all the data points, then divide by the total number of data points. This can be expressed using *summation notation* as:

$$\bar{X} = \frac{x_1 + x_2 + x_3 + \cdots + x_n}{n} = \frac{1}{n}\sum_{i=1}^{n} x_i$$

For example, suppose that in a class of 10 students, the scores on a test were 50, 60, 65, 65, 75, 80, 85, 85, 90, 100. Therefore, the average test score will be $\frac{1}{10}(50 + 60 + 65 + 65 + 75 + 80 + 85 + 85 + 90 + 100) = 75.5$.

The mean is a useful number if the distribution of data is normal (more on this later), which roughly means that the frequency of different outcomes has a single peak and is roughly equally distributed on both sides of that peak. However, it is less useful in some cases where the data might be split or where there are some *outliers*. Outliers are data points that are far from the rest of the data. For example, suppose there are 90 employees and 10 executives at a company. The executives make $1000 per hour, and the employees make $10 per hour. Therefore, the average pay rate will be $\frac{1000 \cdot 10 + 10 \cdot 90}{100} = 109$, or $109 per hour. In this case, this average is not very descriptive.

Another useful measurement is the *median*. In a data set X consisting of data points $x_1, x_2, x_3, \ldots x_n$, the median is the point in the middle. The middle refers to the point where half the data comes before it and half comes after, when the data is recorded in numerical order. If n is odd, then the median is $x_{\frac{n+1}{2}}$. If n is even, it is defined as $\frac{1}{2}\left(x_{\frac{n}{2}} + x_{\frac{n}{2}+1}\right)$, the mean of the two data points closest to the middle of the data points. In the previous example of test scores, the two middle points are 75 and 80. Since there is no single point, the average of these two scores needs to be found. The average is $\frac{75+80}{2} = 77.5$. The median is generally a good value to use if there are a few outliers in the data. It prevents those outliers from affecting the "middle" value as much as when using the mean.

Since an outlier is a data point that is far from most of the other data points in a data set, this means an outlier also is any point that is far from the median of the data set. The outliers can have a substantial effect on the mean of a data set, but usually do not change the median or mode, or do not change them by a large quantity. For example, consider the data set (3, 5, 6, 6, 6, 8). This has a median of 6 and a mode of 6, with a mean of $\frac{34}{6} \approx 5.67$. Now, suppose a new data point of 1000 is added so that the data set is now (3, 5, 6, 6, 6, 8, 1000). This does not change the median or mode, which are both still 6. However, the average is now $\frac{1034}{7}$, which is approximately 147.7. In this case, the median and mode will be better descriptions for most of the data points.

The reason for outliers in a given data set is a complicated problem. It is sometimes the result of an error by the experimenter, but often they are perfectly valid data points that must be taken into consideration.

One additional measure to define for X is the *mode*. This is the data point that appears more frequently. If two or more data points all tie for the most frequent appearance, then each of them is considered a mode. In the case of the test scores, where the numbers were 50, 60, 65, 65, 75, 80, 85, 85, 90, 100, there are two modes: 65 and 85.

The *first quartile* of a set of data X refers to the largest value from the first ¼ of the data points. In practice, there are sometimes slightly different definitions that can be used, such as the median of the first half of the data points (excluding the median itself if there are an odd number of data points). The term also has a slightly different use: when it is said that a data point lies *in the first quartile*, it means it is less than or equal to the median of the first half of the data points. Conversely, if it lies *at* the first quartile, then it is equal to the first quartile.

When it is said that a data point lies in the *second quartile*, it means it is between the first quartile and the median.

The *third quartile* refers to data that lies between ½ and ¾ of the way through the data set. Again, there are various methods for defining this precisely, but the simplest way is to include all of the data that lie between the median and the median of the top half of the data.

Data that lies in the *fourth quartile* refers to all of the data above the third quartile.

Percentiles may be defined in a similar manner to quartiles. Generally, this is defined in the following manner:

If a data point lies *in the n-th percentile*, this means it lies in the range of the first $n\%$ of the data.

If a data point lies *at* the n-th percentile, then it means that $n\%$ of the data lies below this data point.

Given a data set X consisting of data points $(x_1, x_2, x_3, \ldots x_n)$, the *variance* of X is defined to be:

$$\frac{\sum_{i=1}^{n}(x_i - \bar{X})^2}{n}$$

This means that the variance of X is the average of the squares of the differences between each data point and the mean of X.

Given a data set X consisting of data points $(x_1, x_2, x_3, \ldots x_n)$, the *standard deviation* of X is defined to be

$$S_x = \sqrt{\frac{\sum_{i=1}^{n}(x_i - \bar{X})^2}{n}}$$

In other words, the standard deviation is the square root of the variance.

Both the variance and the standard deviation are measures of how much the data tend to be spread out. When the standard deviation is low, the data points are mostly clustered around the mean. When the standard deviation is high, this generally indicates that the data are quite spread out, or else that there are a few substantial outliers.

As a simple example, compute the standard deviation for the data set (1, 3, 3, 5). First, compute the mean, which will be $\frac{1+3+3+5}{4} = \frac{12}{4} = 3$. Now, find the variance of X with the formula: $\sum_{i=1}^{4}(x_i - \bar{X})^2 = (1-3)^2 + (3-3)^2 + (5-3)^2 = -2^2 + 0^2 + 0^2 + 2^2 = 8$. Therefore, the variance is $\frac{8}{4} = 2$. Taking the square root, the standard deviation will be $\sqrt{2}$.

Note that the standard deviation only depends upon the mean, not upon the median or mode(s). Generally, if there are multiple modes that are far apart from one another, the standard deviation will be high. A high standard deviation does not always mean there are multiple modes, however.

Describing a Set of Data

A set of data can be described in terms of its center, spread, shape and any unusual features. The center of a data set can be measured by its mean, median, or mode. The spread of a data set refers to how far the data points are from the center (mean or median). The spread can be measured by the range or the quartiles and interquartile range. A data set with data points clustered around the center will have a small spread. A data set covering a wide range will have a large spread.

When a data set is displayed as a histogram or frequency distribution plot, the shape indicates if a sample is normally distributed, symmetrical, or has measures of skewness or kurtosis. When graphed, a data set with a normal distribution will resemble a bell curve.

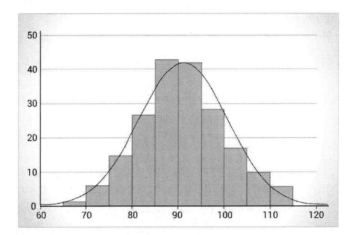

If the data set is symmetrical, each half of the graph when divided at the center is a mirror image of the other. If the graph has fewer data points to the right, the data is skewed right. If it has fewer data points to the left, the data is skewed left.

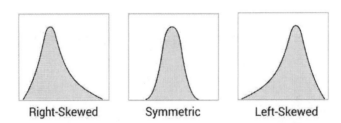

Right-Skewed   Symmetric   Left-Skewed

Kurtosis is a measure of whether the data is heavy-tailed with a high number of outliers, or light-tailed with a low number of outliers.

A description of a data set should include any unusual features such as gaps or outliers. A gap is a span within the range of the data set containing no data points. An outlier is a data point with a value either extremely large or extremely small when compared to the other values in the set.

Common Charts and Graphs

A set of data can be visually displayed in various forms allowing for quick identification of characteristics of the set. Histograms, such as the one shown below, display the number of data points (vertical axis) that fall into given intervals (horizontal axis) across the range of the set. The histogram below displays the heights of black cherry trees in a certain city park. Each rectangle represents the number of trees with heights between a given five-point span. For example, the furthest bar to the right indicates that two trees are between 85 and 90 feet. Histograms can describe the center, spread, shape, and any unusual characteristics of a data set.

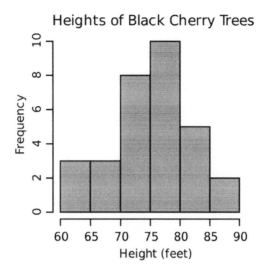

A box plot, also called a box-and-whisker plot, divides the data points into four groups and displays the five-number summary for the set, as well as any outliers. The five-number summary consists of:

- The lower extreme: the lowest value that is not an outlier
- The higher extreme: the highest value that is not an outlier
- The median of the set: also referred to as the second quartile or Q_2
- The first quartile or Q_1: the median of values below Q_2
- The third quartile or Q_3: the median of values above Q_2

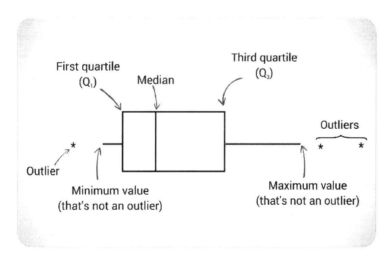

Suppose the box plot displays IQ scores for 12th grade students at a given school. The five number summary of the data consists of: lower extreme (67); upper extreme (127); Q_2 or median (100); Q_1 (91); Q_3 (108); and outliers (135 and 140). Although all data points are not known from the plot, the points are divided into four quartiles each, including 25% of the data points. Therefore, 25% of students scored between 67 and 91, 25% scored between 91 and 100, 25% scored between 100 and 108, and 25% scored between 108 and 127. These percentages include the normal values for the set and exclude the outliers. This information is useful when comparing a given score with the rest of the scores in the set.

A scatter plot is a mathematical diagram that visually displays the relationship or connection between two variables. The independent variable is placed on the *x*-axis, or horizontal axis, and the dependent variable is placed on the *y*-axis, or vertical axis. When visually examining the points on the graph, if the points model a linear relationship, or a line of best-fit can be drawn through the points with the points relatively close on either side, then a correlation exists. If the line of best-fit has a positive slope (rises from left to right), then the variables have a positive correlation. If the line of best-fit has a negative slope (falls from left to right), then the variables have a negative correlation. If a line of best-fit cannot be drawn, then no correlation exists. A positive or negative correlation can be categorized as strong or weak, depending on how closely the points are graphed around the line of best-fit.

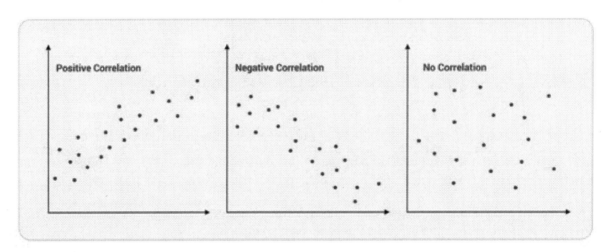

Graphical Representation of Data

Various graphs can be used to visually represent a given set of data. Each type of graph requires a different method of arranging data points and different calculations of the data. To construct a histogram, the range of the data points is divided into equal intervals. The frequency for each interval is then determined, which reveals how many points fall into each interval. A graph is constructed with the vertical axis representing the frequency and the horizontal axis representing the intervals. The lower value of each interval should be labeled along the horizontal axis. Finally, for each interval, a bar is drawn from the lower value of each interval to the lower value of the next interval with a height equal to the frequency of the interval. Because of the intervals, histograms do not have any gaps between bars along the horizontal axis.

To construct a box (or box-and-whisker) plot, the five number summary for the data set is calculated as follows: the second quartile (Q_2) is the median of the set. The first quartile (Q_1) is the median of the values below Q_2. The third quartile (Q_3) is the median of the values above Q_2. The upper extreme is the highest value in the data set if it is not an outlier (greater than 1.5 times the interquartile range $Q_3 - Q_1$). The lower extreme is the least value in the data set if it is not an outlier (more than 1.5 times lower than the interquartile range). To construct the box-and-whisker plot, each value is plotted on a number line, along with any outliers. The *box* consists of Q_1 and Q_3 as its *top* and *bottom* and Q_2 as the dividing line inside the box. The *whiskers* extend from the lower extreme to Q_1 and from Q_3 to the upper extreme.

Box Plot

A scatter plot displays the relationship between two variables. Values for the independent variable, typically denoted by *x*, are paired with values for the dependent variable, typically denoted by *y*. Each set of corresponding values are written as an ordered pair (*x, y*). To construct the graph, a coordinate grid is labeled with the *x*-axis representing the independent variable and the *y*-axis representing the dependent variable. Each ordered pair is graphed.

Like a scatter plot, a line graph compares variables that change continuously, typically over time. Paired data values (ordered pair) are plotted on a coordinate grid with the *x*- and *y*-axis representing the variables. A line is drawn from each point to the next, going from left to right. The line graph below displays cell phone use for given years (two variables) for men, women, and both sexes (three data sets).

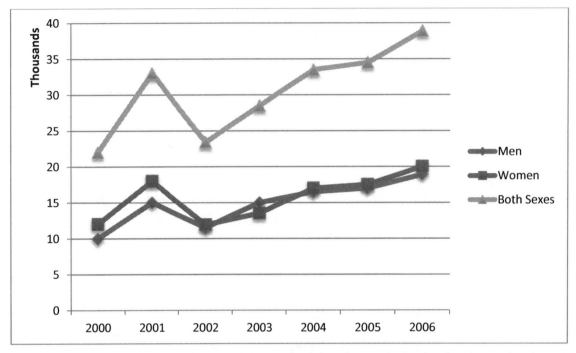

A line plot, also called dot plot, displays the frequency of data (numerical values) on a number line. To construct a line plot, a number line is used that includes all unique data values. It is marked with x's or dots above the value the number of times that the value occurs in the data set.

% Conformance to Goal

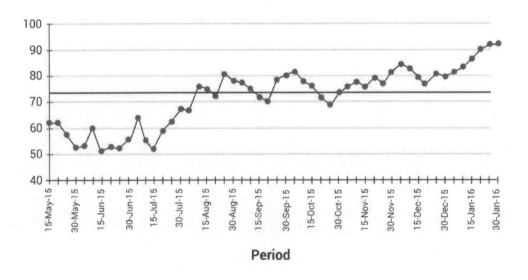

Period

A *bar graph* is a diagram in which the quantity of items within a specific classification is represented by the height of a rectangle. Each type of classification is represented by a rectangle of equal width. Here is an example of a bar graph:

A circle graph, also called a pie chart, shows categorical data with each category representing a percentage of the whole data set. To make a circle graph, the percent of the data set for each category must be determined. To do so, the frequency of the category is divided by the total number of data points and converted to a percent. For example, if 80 people were asked what their favorite sport is and

20 responded basketball, basketball makes up 25% of the data ($\frac{20}{80}=.25=25\%$). Each category in a data set is represented by a *slice* of the circle proportionate to its percentage of the whole.

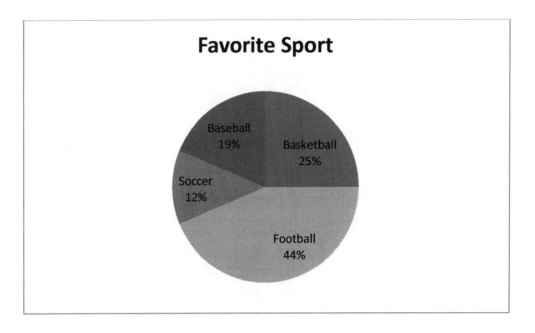

Probability

Given a set of possible outcomes *X*, a *probability distribution* on *X* is a function that assigns a probability to each possible outcome. If the outcomes are $(x_1, x_2, x_3, \dots x_n)$, and the probability distribution is *p*, then the following rules are applied.

- $0 \leq p(x_i) \leq 1$, for any i.

- $\sum_{i=1}^{n} p(x_i) = 1$.

In other words, the probability of a given outcome must be between zero and 1, while the total probability must be 1.

If $p(x_i)$ is constant, then this is called a *uniform probability distribution*, and $p(x_i) = \frac{1}{n}$. For example, on a six-sided die, the probability of each of the six outcomes will be $\frac{1}{6}$.

If seeking the probability of an outcome occurring in some specific range *A* of possible outcomes, written $P(A)$, add up the probabilities for each outcome in that range. For example, consider a six-sided die, and figure the probability of getting a 3 or lower when it is rolled. The possible rolls are 1, 2, 3, 4, 5, and 6. So, to get a 3 or lower, a roll a 1, 2, or 3 must be completed. The probabilities of each of these is $\frac{1}{6}$, so add these to get $p(1) + p(2) + p(3) = \frac{1}{6} + \frac{1}{6} + \frac{1}{6} = \frac{1}{2}$.

An outcome occasionally lies within some range of possibilities *B*, and the probability that the outcomes also lie within some set of possibilities *A* needs to be figured. This is called a *conditional probability*. It is written as $P(A|B)$, which is read "the probability of *A* given *B*." The general formula for computing conditional probabilities is $P(A|B) = \frac{P(A \cap B)}{P(B)}$.

However, when dealing with uniform probability distributions, simplify this a bit. Write $|A|$ to indicate the number of outcomes in A. Then, for uniform probability distributions, write $P(A|B) = \frac{|A \cap B|}{|B|}$ (recall that $A \cap B$ means "A intersect B," and consists of all of the outcomes that lie in both A and B). This means that all possible outcomes do not need to be known. To see why this formula works, suppose that the set of outcomes X is $(x_1, x_2, x_3, \ldots x_n)$, so that $|X| = n$. Then, for a uniform probability distribution, $P(A) = \frac{|A|}{n}$. However, this means $(A|B) = \frac{P(A \cap B)}{P(B)} = \frac{\frac{|A \cap B|}{n}}{\frac{|B|}{n}} = \frac{|A \cap B|}{|B|}$, since the n's cancel out.

For example, suppose a die is rolled and it is known that it will land between 1 and 4. However, how many sides the die has is unknown. Figure the probability that the die is rolled higher than 2. To figure this, $P(3)$ or $P(4)$ does not need to be determined, or any of the other probabilities, since it is known that a fair die has a uniform probability distribution. Therefore, apply the formula $\frac{|A \cap B|}{|B|}$. So, in this case B is $(1, 2, 3, 4)$ and $A \cap B$ is $(3, 4)$. Therefore $\frac{|A \cap B|}{|B|} = \frac{2}{4} = \frac{1}{2}$.

Conditional probability is an important concept because, in many situations, the likelihood of one outcome can differ radically depending on how something else comes out. The probability of passing a test given that one has studied all of the material is generally much higher than the probability of passing a test given that one has not studied at all. The probability of a person having heart trouble is much lower if that person exercises regularly. The probability that a college student will graduate is higher when his or her SAT scores are higher, and so on. For this reason, there are many people who are interested in conditional probabilities.

Note that in some practical situations, changing the order of the conditional probabilities can make the outcome very different. For example, the probability that a person with heart trouble has exercised regularly is quite different than the probability that a person who exercises regularly will have heart trouble. The probability of a person receiving a military-only award, given that he or she is or was a soldier, is generally not very high, but the probability that a person being or having been a soldier, given that he or she received a military-only award, is 1.

However, in some cases, the outcomes do not influence one another this way. If the probability of A is the same regardless of whether B is given; that is, if $P(A|B) = P(A)$, then A and B are considered *independent*. In this case, $P(A|B) = \frac{P(A \cap B)}{P(B)} = P(A)$, so $P(A \cap B) = P(A)P(B)$. In fact, if $P(A \cap B) = P(A)P(B)$, it can be determined that $P(A|B) = P(A)$ and $P(A|B) = P(B)$ by working backward. Therefore, B is also independent of A.

An example of something being independent can be seen in rolling dice. In this case, consider a red die and a green die. It is expected that when the dice are rolled, the outcome of the green die should not depend in any way on the outcome of the red die. Or, to take another example, if the same die is rolled repeatedly, then the next number rolled should not depend on which numbers have been rolled previously. Similarly, if a coin is flipped, then the next flip's outcome does not depend on the outcomes of previous flips.

This can sometimes be counter-intuitive, since when rolling a die or flipping a coin, there can be a streak of surprising results. If, however, it is known that the die or coin is fair, then these results are just the result of the fact that over long periods of time, it is very likely that some unlikely streaks of outcomes will occur. Therefore, avoid making the mistake of thinking that when considering a series of independent outcomes, a particular outcome is "due to happen" simply because a surprising series of outcomes has already been seen.

There is a second type of common mistake that people tend to make when reasoning about statistical outcomes: the idea that when something of low probability happens, this is surprising. It would be surprising that something with low probability happened after just one attempt. However, with so much happening all at once, it is easy to see at least something happen in a way that seems to have a very low probability. In fact, a lottery is a good example. The odds of winning a lottery are very small, but the odds that somebody wins the lottery each week are actually fairly high. Therefore, no one should be surprised when some low probability things happen.

The *addition rule* for probabilities states that the probability of A or B happening is $P(A \cup B) = P(A) + P(B) - P(A \cap B)$. Note that the subtraction of $P(A \cap B)$ must be performed, or else it would result in double counting any outcomes that lie in both A and in B. For example, suppose that a 20-sided die is being rolled. Fred bets that the outcome will be greater than 10, while Helen bets that it will be greater than 4 but less than 15. What is the probability that at least one of them is correct?

We apply the rule $P(A \cup B) = P(A) + P(B) - P(A \cap B)$, where A is that outcome x is in the range $x > 10$, and B is that outcome x is in the range $4 < x < 15$. $P(A) = 10 \cdot \frac{1}{20} = \frac{1}{2}$. $P(B) = 10 \cdot \frac{1}{20} = \frac{1}{2}$. $P(A \cap B)$ can be computed by noting that $A \cap B$ means the outcome x is in the range $10 < x < 15$, so $P(A \cap B) = 4 \cdot \frac{1}{20} = \frac{1}{5}$. Therefore, $P(A \cup B) = P(A) + P(B) - P(A \cap B) = \frac{1}{2} + \frac{1}{2} - \frac{1}{5} = \frac{4}{5}$.

Note that in this particular example, we could also have directly reasoned about the set of possible outcomes $A \cup B$, by noting that this would mean that x must be in the range $5 \le x$. However, this is not always the case, depending on the given information.

The *multiplication rule* for probabilities states the probability of A and B both happening is $P(A \cap B) = P(A)P(B|A)$. As an example, suppose that when Jamie wears black pants, there is a ½ probability that she wears a black shirt as well, and that she wears black pants ¾ of the time. What is the probability that she is wearing both a black shirt and black pants?

To figure this, use the above formula, where A will be "Jamie is wearing black pants," while B will be "Jamie is wearing a black shirt." It is known that $P(A)$ is ¾. It is also known that $P(B|A) = \frac{1}{2}$. Multiplying the two, the probability that she is wearing both black pants and a black shirt is $P(A)P(B|A) = \frac{3}{4} \cdot \frac{1}{2} = \frac{3}{8}$.

Measurement and Geometry

Measurement

The United States customary system and the metric system each consist of distinct units to measure lengths and volume of liquids. The U.S. customary units for length, from smallest to largest, are: inch (in), foot (ft), yard (yd), and mile (mi). The metric units for length, from smallest to largest, are: millimeter (mm), centimeter (cm), decimeter (dm), meter (m), and kilometer (km). The relative size of each unit of length is shown below.

U.S. Customary	Metric	Conversion
12in = 1ft	10mm = 1cm	1in = 254cm
36in = 3ft = 1yd	10cm = 1dm(decimeter)	1m ≈ 3.28ft ≈ 1.09yd
5,280ft = 1,760yd = 1mi	100cm = 10dm = 1m	1mi ≈ 1.6km
	1000m = 1km	

The U.S. customary units for volume of liquids, from smallest to largest, are: fluid ounces (fl oz), cup (c), pint (pt), quart (qt), and gallon (gal). The metric units for volume of liquids, from smallest to largest, are: milliliter (mL), centiliter (cL), deciliter (dL), liter (L), and kiloliter (kL). The relative size of each unit of liquid volume is shown below.

U.S. Customary	Metric	Conversion
8fl oz = 1c	10mL = 1cL	1pt ≈ 0.473L
2c = 1pt	10cL = 1dL	1L ≈ 1.057qt
4c = 2pt = 1qt	1,000mL = 100cL = 10dL = 1L	1gal ≈ 3,785L
4qt = 1gal	1,000L = 1kL	

The U.S. customary system measures weight (how strongly Earth is pulling on an object) in the following units, from least to greatest: ounce (oz), pound (lb), and ton. The metric system measures mass (the quantity of matter within an object) in the following units, from least to greatest: milligram (mg), centigram (cg), gram (g), kilogram (kg), and metric ton (MT). The relative sizes of each unit of weight and mass are shown below.

U.S. Measures of Weight	Metric Measures of Mass
16oz = 1lb	10mg = 1cg
2,000lb = 1 ton	100cg = 1g
	1,000g = 1kg
	1,000kg = 1MT

Note that weight and mass DO NOT measure the same thing.

Time is measured in the following units, from shortest to longest: second (sec), minute (min), hour (h), day (d), week (wk), month (mo), year (yr), decade, century, millennium. The relative sizes of each unit of time is shown below.

- 60sec = 1min
- 60min = 1h
- 24hr = 1d

- 7d = 1wk
- 52wk = 1yr
- 12mo = 1yr
- 10yr = 1 decade
- 100yrs = 1 century
- 1,000yrs = 1 millennium

- When working with different systems of measurement, conversion from one unit to another may be necessary. The conversion rate must be known to convert units. One method for converting units is to write and solve a proportion. The arrangement of values in a proportion is extremely important. Suppose that a problem requires converting 20 fluid ounces to cups. To do so, a proportion can be written using the conversion rate of 8fl oz = 1c with x representing the missing value. The proportion can be written in any of the following ways:

- $\dfrac{1}{8} = \dfrac{x}{20} \left(\dfrac{c\ for\ conversion}{fl\ oz\ for\ conversion} = \dfrac{unknown\ c}{fl\ oz\ given} \right); \dfrac{8}{1} = \dfrac{20}{x} \left(\dfrac{fl\ oz\ for\ conversion}{c\ for\ conversion} = \dfrac{fl\ oz\ given}{unknown\ c} \right);$

- $\dfrac{1}{x} = \dfrac{8}{20} \left(\dfrac{c\ for\ conversion}{unknown\ c} = \dfrac{fl\ oz\ for\ conversion}{fl\ oz\ given} \right); \dfrac{x}{1} = \dfrac{20}{8} \left(\dfrac{unknown\ c}{c\ for\ conversion} = \dfrac{fl\ oz\ given}{fl\ oz\ for\ conversion} \right)$

- To solve a proportion, the ratios are cross-multiplied and the resulting equation is solved. When cross-multiplying, all four proportions above will produce the same equation: $(8)(x) = (20)(1) \rightarrow 8x = 20$. Dividing by 8 to isolate the variable x, the result is $x = 2.5$. The variable x represented the unknown number of cups. Therefore, the conclusion is that 20 fluid ounces converts (is equal) to 2.5 cups.

- Sometimes converting units requires writing and solving more than one proportion. Suppose an exam question asks to determine how many hours are in 2 weeks. Without knowing the conversion rate between hours and weeks, this can be determined knowing the conversion rates between weeks and days, and between days and hours. First, weeks are converted to days, then days are converted to hours. To convert from weeks to days, the following proportion can be written $\dfrac{7}{1} = \dfrac{x}{2} \left(\dfrac{days\ conversion}{weeks\ conversion} = \dfrac{days\ unknown}{weeks\ given} \right)$.

- Cross-multiplying produces: $(7)(2) = (x)(1) \rightarrow 14 = x$. Therefore, 2 weeks is equal to 14 days. Next, a proportion is written to convert 14 days to hours: $\dfrac{24}{1} = \dfrac{x}{14} \left(\dfrac{conversion\ hours}{conversion\ days} = \dfrac{unknown\ hours}{given\ days} \right)$. Cross-multiplying produces: $(24)(14) = (x)(1) \rightarrow 336 = x$. Therefore, the answer is that there are 336 hours in 2 weeks.

Lines and Planes

The basic unit of geometry is a point. These are locations on the plane that have no width or breadth. The position of a point is indicated with a dot and usually named with a single uppercase letter, such as point *A* or point *T*. A point is a place, not a thing, and therefore has no dimensions or size. A set of points that lies on the same line is called collinear. A set of points that lies on the same plane is called coplanar.

The image above displays point *A*, point *B*, and point *C*.

Any pair of points *A*, *B* on the plane will determine a unique straight line between them. This line is denoted *AB*. Sometimes to emphasize a line is being considered, this will be written as $\overleftrightarrow{AB}$.

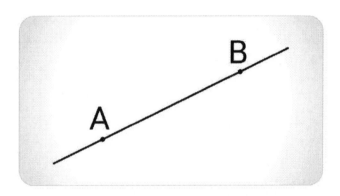

If the Cartesian coordinates for *A* and *B* are known, then the distance $d(A, B)$ along the line between them can be measured using the *Pythagorean formula*, which states that if $A = (x_1, y_1)$ and $B = (x_2, y_2)$, then the distance between them is $d(A, B) = \sqrt{(x_2 - x_1)^2 + (y_2 - y_1)^2}$.

The part of a line that lies between *A* and *B* is called a *line segment*. It has two endpoints, one at *A* and one at *B*. *Rays* also can be formed. Given points *A* and *B*, a *ray* is the portion of a line that starts at one of these points, passes through the other, and keeps on going. Therefore, a ray has a single endpoint, but the other end goes off to infinity.

Two lines are considered parallel to each other if, while extending infinitely, they will never intersect (or meet). Parallel lines point in the same direction and are always the same distance apart. Two lines are considered perpendicular if they intersect to form right angles. Right angles are 90°. Typically, a small box is drawn at the intersection point to indicate the right angle.

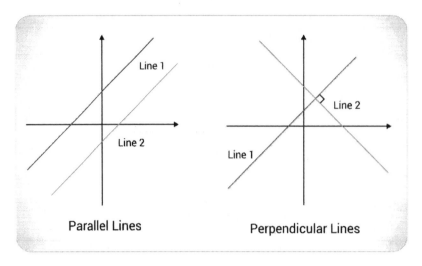

Line 1 is parallel to line 2 in the left image and is written as line 1 || line 2. Line 1 is perpendicular to line 2 in the right image and is written as line 1 ⊥ line 2.

<u>Angles</u>
An angle consists of two rays that have a common endpoint. This common endpoint is called the vertex of the angle. The two rays can be called sides of the angle. The angle below has a vertex at point *B* and the sides consist of ray *BA* and ray *BC*. An angle can be named in three ways:

1. Using the vertex and a point from each side, with the vertex letter in the middle.
2. Using only the vertex. This can only be used if it is the only angle with that vertex.
3. Using a number that is written inside the angle.

The angle below can be written ∠*ABC* (read angle *ABC*), ∠*CBA*, ∠*B*, or ∠1.

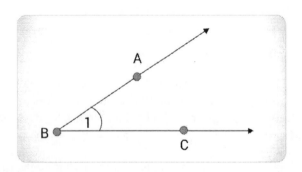

An angle divides a plane, or flat surface, into three parts: the angle itself, the interior (inside) of the angle, and the exterior (outside) of the angle. The figure below shows point *M* on the interior of the angle and point *N* on the exterior of the angle.

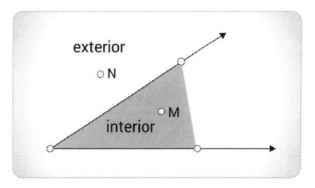

Angles can be measured in units called degrees, with the symbol °. The degree measure of an angle is between 0° and 180° and can be obtained by using a protractor.

A straight angle (or simply a line) measures exactly 180°. A right angle's sides meet at the vertex to create a square corner. A right angle measures exactly 90° and is typically indicated by a box drawn in the interior of the angle. An acute angle has an interior that is narrower than a right angle. The measure of an acute angle is any value less than 90° and greater than 0°. For example, 89.9°, 47°, 12°, and 1°. An obtuse angle has an interior that is wider than a right angle. The measure of an obtuse angle is any value greater than 90° but less than 180°. For example, 90.1°, 110°, 150°, and 179.9°.

- Acute angles: Less than 90°
- Obtuse angles: Greater than 90°
- Right angles: 90°
- Straight angles: 180°

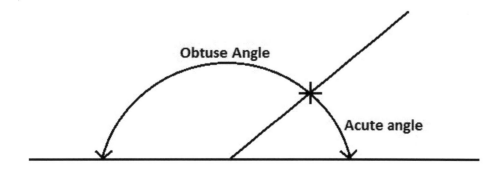

Adjacent angles are two side-by-side angles formed from the same ray that have the same endpoint.

Polygons

A *polygon* is a closed figure (meaning it divides the plane into an inside and an outside) consisting of a collection of line segments between points. These points are called the *vertices* of the polygon. These line segments must not overlap one another. Note that the number of sides is equal to the number of angles, or vertices of the polygon. The angles between line segments meeting one another in the polygon are called *interior angles*.

A *regular polygon* is a polygon whose edges are all the same length and whose interior angles are all of equal measure.

Polygons can be classified by the number of sides (also equal to the number of angles) they have. The following are the names of polygons with a given number of sides or angles:

# of sides	3	4	5	6	7	8	9	10
Name of polygon	Triangle	Quadrilateral	Pentagon	Hexagon	Septagon (or heptagon)	Octagon	Nonagon	Decagon

A *triangle* is a polygon with three sides. A *quadrilateral* is a polygon with four sides.

Quadrilaterals can be further classified according to their sides and angles. A quadrilateral with exactly one pair of parallel sides is called a trapezoid. A quadrilateral that shows both pairs of opposite sides parallel is a parallelogram. Parallelograms include rhombuses, rectangles, and squares. A rhombus has four equal sides. A rectangle has four equal angles (90° each). A square has four 90° angles and four equal sides. Therefore, a square is both a rhombus and a rectangle.

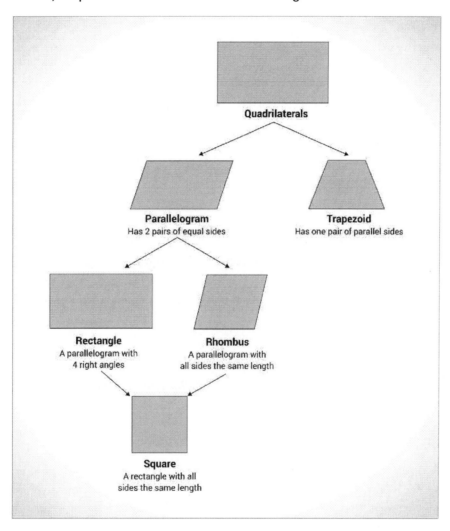

Triangles
A *right triangle* is a triangle that has one 90° angle.

The sum of the interior angles of any triangle must add up to 180°.

An *isosceles triangle* is a triangle in which two of the sides are the same length. In this case, it will always have two congruent interior angles. If a triangle has two congruent interior angles, it will always be isosceles.

An *equilateral triangle* is a triangle whose sides are all the same length and whose angles are all equivalent to one another, equal to 60°. Equilateral triangles are examples of regular polygons. Note that equilateral triangles are also isosceles. A triangle with no equal sides or angles is a scalene triangle.

Angles that add up to 90 degrees are *complementary*. Within a right triangle, two complementary angles exist because the third angle is always 90 degrees.

Pythagorean Theorem

The Pythagorean theorem is an important result in geometry. It states that for right triangles, the sum of the squares of the two shorter sides will be equal to the square of the longest side (also called the *hypotenuse*). The longest side will always be the side opposite to the 90° angle. If this side is called c, and the other two sides are a and b, then the Pythagorean theorem states that $c^2 = a^2 + b^2$. Since lengths are always positive, this also can be written as $c = \sqrt{a^2 + b^2}$.

A diagram to show the parts of a triangle using the Pythagorean theorem is below.

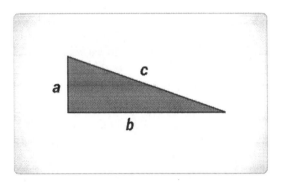

As an example of the theorem, suppose that Shirley has a rectangular field that is 5 feet wide and 12 feet long, and she wants to split it in half using a fence that goes from one corner to the opposite corner. How long will this fence need to be? To figure this out, note that this makes the field into two right triangles, whose hypotenuse will be the fence dividing it in half. Therefore, the fence length will be given by $\sqrt{5^2 + 12^2} = \sqrt{169} = 13$ feet long.

Transformations of a Plane

Given a figure drawn on a plane, many changes can be made to that figure, including *rotation*, *translation*, and *reflection*. Rotations turn the figure about a point, translations slide the figure, and reflections flip the figure over a specified line. When performing these transformations, the original figure is called the *pre-image*, and the figure after transformation is called the *image*.

More specifically, *translation* means that all points in the figure are moved in the same direction by the same distance. In other words, the figure is slid in some fixed direction. Of course, while the entire figure is slid by the same distance, this does not change any of the measurements of the figures involved. The result will have the same distances and angles as the original figure.

In terms of Cartesian coordinates, a translation means a shift of each of the original points (x, y) by a fixed amount in the x and y directions, to become $(x + a, y + b)$.

Another procedure that can be performed is called *reflection*. To do this, a line in the plane is specified, called the *line of reflection*. Then, take each point and flip it over the line so that it is the same distance from the line but on the opposite side of it. This does not change any of the distances or angles involved, but it does reverse the order in which everything appears.

To reflect something over the x-axis, the points (x, y) are sent to $(x, -y)$. To reflect something over the y-axis, the points (x, y) are sent to the points $(-x, y)$. Flipping over other lines is not something easy to express in Cartesian coordinates. However, by drawing the figure and the line of reflection, the distance to the line and the original points can be used to find the reflected figure.

Example: Reflect this triangle with vertices (-1, 0), (2, 1), and (2, 0) over the y-axis. The pre-image is shown below.

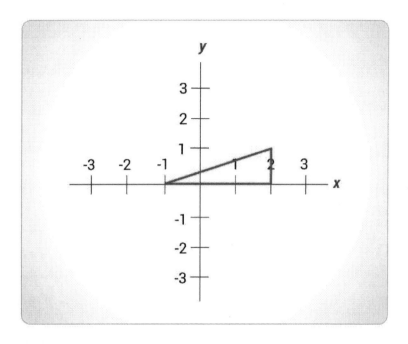

To do this, flip the x values of the points involved to the negatives of themselves, while keeping the y values the same. The image is shown here.

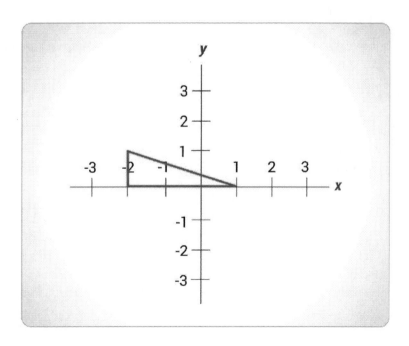

The new vertices will be (1, 0), (-2, 1), and (-2, 0).

Another procedure that does not change the distances and angles in a figure is *rotation*. In this procedure, pick a center point, then rotate every vertex along a circle around that point by the same angle. This procedure is also not easy to express in Cartesian coordinates, and this is not a requirement on this test. However, as with reflections, it's helpful to draw the figures and see what the result of the rotation would look like. This transformation can be performed using a compass and protractor.

Each one of these transformations can be performed on the coordinate plane without changes to the original dimensions or angles.

If two figures in the plane involve the same distances and angles, they are called *congruent figures*. In other words, two figures are congruent when they go from one form to another through reflection, rotation, and translation, or a combination of these.

Remember that rotation and translation will give back a new figure that is identical to the original figure, but reflection will give back a mirror image of it.

To recognize that a figure has undergone a rotation, check to see that the figure has not been changed into a mirror image, but that its orientation has changed (that is, whether the parts of the figure now form different angles with the x and y axes).

To recognize that a figure has undergone a translation, check to see that the figure has not been changed into a mirror image, and that the orientation remains the same.

To recognize that a figure has undergone a reflection, check to see that the new figure is a mirror image of the old figure.

Keep in mind that sometimes a combination of translations, reflections, and rotations may be performed on a figure.

A *dilation* is a transformation that preserves angles, but not distances. This can be thought of as stretching or shrinking a figure. If a dilation makes figures larger, it is called an *enlargement*. If a dilation makes figures smaller, it is called a *reduction*. The easiest example is to dilate around the origin. In this case, multiply the x and y coordinates by a *scale factor*, k, sending points (x, y) to (kx, ky).

Note that after a dilation, the distances between the vertices of the figure will have changed, but the angles remain the same. The two figures that are obtained by dilation, along with possibly translation, rotation, and reflection, are all *similar* to one another. Another way to think of this is that similar figures have the same number of vertices and edges, and their angles are all the same. Similar figures have the same basic shape, but are different in size.

Using the types of transformations above, if an object can undergo these changes and not appear to have changed, then the figure is symmetrical. If an object can be split in half by a line and flipped over that line to lie directly on top of itself, it is said to have *line symmetry*. An example of both types of figures is seen below.

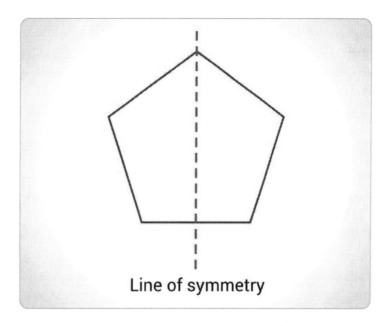

Line of symmetry

Similar Figures

Sometimes, two figures are similar, meaning they have the same basic shape and the same interior angles, but they have different dimensions. If the ratio of two corresponding sides is known, then that ratio, or scale factor, holds true for all of the dimensions of the new figure.

Here is an example of applying this principle. Suppose that Lara is 5 feet tall and is standing 30 feet from the base of a light pole, and her shadow is 6 feet long. How high is the light on the pole? To figure this, it helps to make a sketch of the situation:

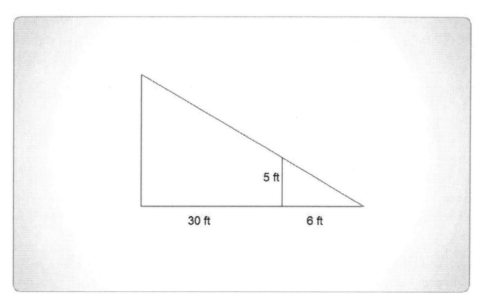

The light pole is the left side of the triangle. Lara is the 5-foot vertical line. Notice that there are two right triangles here, and that they have all the same angles as one another. Therefore, they form similar triangles. So, figure the ratio of proportionality between them.

The bases of these triangles are known. The small triangle, formed by Lara and her shadow, has a base of 6 feet. The large triangle, formed by the light pole along with the line from the base of the pole out to the end of Lara's shadow is $30 + 6 = 36$ feet long. So, the ratio of the big triangle to the little triangle will be $\frac{36}{6} = 6$. The height of the little triangle is 5 feet. Therefore, the height of the big triangle will be $6 \cdot 5 = 30$ feet, meaning that the light is 30 feet up the pole.

Notice that the perimeter of a figure changes by the ratio of proportionality between two similar figures, but the area changes by the *square* of the ratio. This is because if the length of one side is doubled, the area is quadrupled.

As an example, suppose two rectangles are similar, but the edges of the second rectangle are three times longer than the edges of the first rectangle. The area of the first rectangle is 10 square inches. How much more area does the second rectangle have than the first?

To answer this, note that the area of the second rectangle is $3^2 = 9$ times the area of the first rectangle, which is 10 square inches. Therefore, the area of the second rectangle is going to be $9 \cdot 10 = 90$ square inches. This means it has $90 - 10 = 80$ square inches more area than the first rectangle.

As a second example, suppose X and Y are similar right triangles. The hypotenuse of X is 4 inches. The area of Y is $\frac{1}{4}$ the area of X. What is the hypotenuse of Y?

First, realize the area has changed by a factor of $\frac{1}{4}$. The area changes by a factor that is the *square* of the ratio of changes in lengths, so the ratio of the lengths is the square root of the ratio of areas. That means that the ratio of lengths must be is $\sqrt{\frac{1}{4}} = \frac{1}{2}$, and the hypotenuse of Y must be $\frac{1}{2} \cdot 4 = 2$ inches.

Volumes between similar solids change like the cube of the change in the lengths of their edges. Likewise, if the ratio of the volumes between similar solids is known, the ratio between their lengths is known by finding the cube root of the ratio of their volumes.

For example, suppose there are two similar rectangular pyramids X and Y. The base of X is 1 inch by 2 inches, and the volume of X is 8 inches. The volume of Y is 64 inches. What are the dimensions of the base of Y?

To answer this, first find the ratio of the volume of Y to the volume of X. This will be given by $\frac{64}{8} = 8$. Now the ratio of lengths is the cube root of the ratio of volumes, or $\sqrt[3]{8} = 2$. So, the dimensions of the base of Y must be 2 inches by 4 inches.

Circles

A *circle* can be defined as the set of all points that are the same distance (known as the radius, **r**) from a single point (known as the center of the circle). The center has coordinates (h, k), and any point on the circle can be labelled with coordinates (x, y).

The *circumference* of a circle is the distance traveled by following the edge of the circle for one complete revolution, and the length of the circumference is given by $2\pi r$, where r is the radius of the circle. The formula for circumference is $C = 2\pi r$.

Given two points on the circumference of a circle, the path along the circle between those points is called an *arc* of the circle. For example, the arc between B and C is denoted by a thinner line:

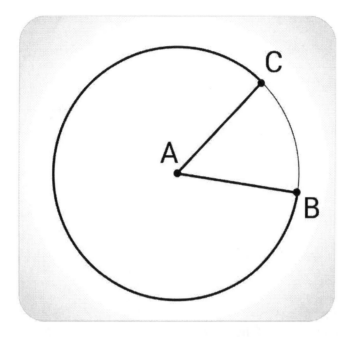

The length of the path along an arc is called the *arc length*. If the circle has radius r, then the arc length is given by multiplying the measure of the angle in radians by the radius of the circle.

The equation used to find the area of a circle is $A = \pi r^2$. For example, if a circle has a radius of 5 centimeters, the area is computed by substituting 5 for the radius: $(5)^2$. Using this reasoning, to find half of the area of a circle, the formula is $A = .5\pi r^2$. Similarly, to find the quarter of an area of a circle, the formula is $A = .25\pi r^2$. To find any fractional area of a circle, a student can use the formula $A = \frac{C}{360}\pi r^2$, where C is the number of degrees of the central angle of the sector. The area of a circle can also be found by using the arc length rather than the degree of the sector. This formula is $A = rs^2$, where s is the arc length and r is the radius of the circle.

Area and Perimeter
The perimeter of a polygon is the distance around the outside of the two-dimensional figure. Perimeter is a one-dimensional measurement and is therefore expressed in linear units such as centimeters (*cm*), feet (*ft*), and miles (*mi*). The perimeter (*P*) of a figure can be calculated by adding together each of the sides.

Properties of certain polygons allow that the perimeter may be obtained by using formulas. A rectangle consists of two sides called the length (*l*), which have equal measures, and two sides called the width (*w*), which have equal measures. Therefore, the perimeter (*P*) of a rectangle can be expressed as P = l + l + w + w. This can be simplified to produce the following formula to find the perimeter of a rectangle: P = 2l + 2w or P = 2(l + w).

A regular polygon is one in which all sides have equal length and all interior angles have equal measures, such as a square and an equilateral triangle. To find the perimeter of a regular polygon, the length of one side is multiplied by the number of sides. For example, to find the perimeter of an equilateral triangle with a side of length of 4 feet, 4 feet is multiplied by 3 (number of sides of a triangle). The perimeter of a regular octagon (8 sides) with a side of length of $\frac{1}{2}$cm is $\frac{1}{2}cm \times 8 = 4cm$.

The area of a polygon is the number of square units needed to cover the interior region of the figure. Area is a two-dimensional measurement. Therefore, area is expressed in square units, such as square centimeters (cm^2), square feet (ft^2), or square miles (mi^2). Regarding the area of a rectangle with sides of length x and y, the area is given by xy. For a triangle with a base of length b and a height of length h, the area is $\frac{1}{2}bh$. To find the area (A) of a parallelogram, the length of the base (b) is multiplied by the length of the height (h) → $A = b \times h$. Similar to triangles, the height of the parallelogram is measured from one base to the other at a 90° angle (or perpendicular).

Area = bh

Perimeter = 2(a + b)

The area of a trapezoid can be calculated using the formula: $A = \frac{1}{2} \times h(b_1 + b_2)$, where h is the height and b_1 and b_2 are the parallel bases of the trapezoid.

$$A = \frac{1}{2}(b_1 + b_2)h$$

The area of a regular polygon can be determined by using its perimeter and the length of the apothem. The apothem is a line from the center of the regular polygon to any of its sides at a right angle. (Note that the perimeter of a regular polygon can be determined given the length of only one side.) The formula for the area (A) of a regular polygon is $A = \frac{1}{2} \times a \times P$, where a is the length of the apothem and P is the perimeter of the figure.

Consider the following regular pentagon:

8 cm

To find the area, the perimeter (P) is calculated first: $8cm \times 5 \to P = 40cm$. Then the perimeter and the apothem are used to find the area (A): $A = \frac{1}{2} \times a \times P \to A = \frac{1}{2} \times (6cm) \times (40cm) \to A = 120cm^2$. Note that the unit is $cm^2 \to cm \times cm = cm^2$.

The area of irregular polygons is found by decomposing, or breaking apart, the figure into smaller shapes. When the area of the smaller shapes is determined, the area of the smaller shapes will produce the area of the original figure when added together. Consider the example below:

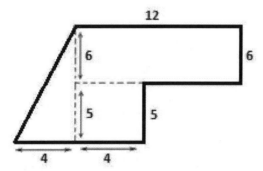

The irregular polygon is decomposed into two rectangles and a triangle. The area of the large rectangles ($A = l \times w \to A = 12 \times 6$) is 72 square units. The area of the small rectangle is 20 square units ($A = 4 \times 5$). The area of the triangle ($A = \frac{1}{2} \times b \times h \to A = \frac{1}{2} \times 4 \times 11$) is 22 square units. The sum of the areas of these figures produces the total area of the original polygon: $A = 72 + 20 + 22 \to A = 114$ square units.

Surface Area and Volume
Geometry in three dimensions is similar to geometry in two dimensions. The main new feature is that three points now define a unique *plane* that passes through each of them. Three dimensional objects can be made by putting together two dimensional figures in different surfaces. Below, some of the possible three dimensional figures will be provided, along with formulas for their volumes and surface areas.

Volume is the capacity of a three-dimensional shape. Volume is useful in determining the space within a certain three-dimensional object. Volume can be calculated for a cube, rectangular prism, cylinder, pyramid, cone, and sphere. By knowing specific dimensions of the objects, the volume of the object is computed with these figures. The units for the volumes of solids can include cubic centimeters, cubic meters, cubic inches, and cubic feet.

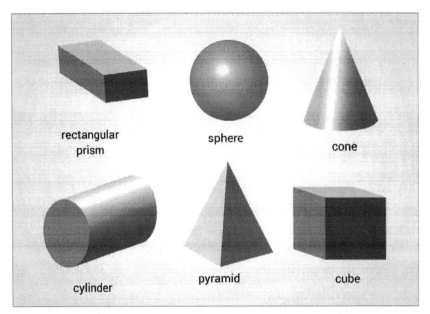

A rectangular prism is a box whose sides are all rectangles meeting at 90° angles. Such a box has three dimensions: length, width, and height. If the length is x, the width is y, and the height is z, then the volume is given by $V = xyz$.

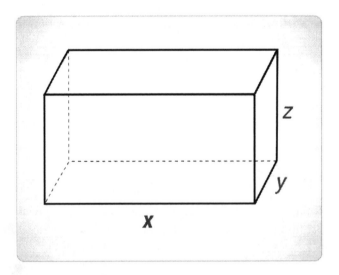

The surface area will be given by computing the surface area of each rectangle and adding them together. There are a total of six rectangles. Two of them have sides of length x and y, two have sides of length y and z, and two have sides of length x and z. Therefore, the total surface area will be given by $SA = 2xy + 2yz + 2xz$.

A *cube* is a special type of rectangular solid in which its length, width, and height are the same. If this length is s, then the formula for the volume of a cube is $V = s \times s \times s$. The surface area of a cube is $SA = 6s^2$.

A *rectangular pyramid* is a figure with a rectangular base and four triangular sides that meet at a single vertex. If the rectangle has sides of length x and y, then the volume will be given by $V = \frac{1}{3}xyh$.

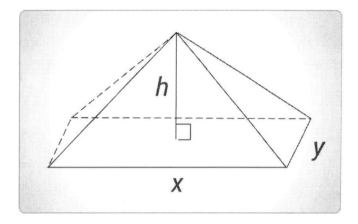

To find the surface area, the dimensions of each triangle need to be known. However, these dimensions can differ depending on the problem in question. Therefore, there is no general formula for calculating total surface area.

A *sphere* is a set of points all of which are equidistant from some central point. It is like a circle, but in three dimensions. The volume of a sphere of radius r is given by $V = \frac{4}{3}\pi r^3$. The surface area is given by $A = 4\pi r^2$.

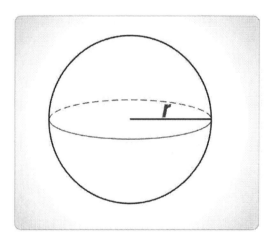

Discovering a cylinder's volume requires the measurement of the cylinder's base, length of the radius, and height. The height of the cylinder can be represented with variable h, and the radius can be represented with variable r.

The formula to find the volume of a cylinder is $\pi r^2 h$. Notice that πr^2 is the formula for the area of a circle. This is because the base of the cylinder is a circle. To calculate the volume of a cylinder, the slices of circles needed to build the entire height of the cylinder are added together. For example, if the radius is 5 feet and the height of the cylinder is 10 feet, the cylinder's volume is calculated by using the following equation: $\pi 5^2 \times 10$. Substituting 3.14 for π, the volume is 785.4 ft³.

Practice Test #1

No Calculator Questions

1. 3.4+2.35+4=
    a. 5.35
    b. 9.2
    c. 9.75
    d. 10.25

2. 6 is 30% of what number?
    a. 18
    b. 20
    c. 24
    d. 26

3. The table below shows the number of books Cameron has read per month over the past year. Use the data from the table to fill in the missing points (March, June, August, and September) on the scatter plot that follows.

Month	Books Read
January	4
February	2
March	5
April	3
May	1
June	5
July	7
August	4
September	1
October	3
November	2
December	6

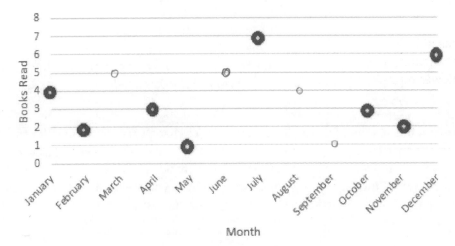

Number of Books Read

4. Pete's Café is a popular breakfast spot for local office workers, who often pick up breakfast for their coworkers. The café is running a special on Monday morning. All customers who spend at least $17.00 on breakfast orders will receive a free donut with their purchase. The table below shows the menu prices for the items. The table that follows shows the orders that seven customers made. Determine the order total for each customer and place a check mark in the appropriate box for those customers whose order exceeds $17.00.

Item	Cost
Coffee	$1.50
Tea	$0.95
Juice	$2.00
Bagel	$1.75
Muffin	$2.50
Donut	$0.75
Fruit Salad	$3.50
Oatmeal	$3.00
Toast	$0.50

Customer	Purchase	Total	Free Donut
Ben	4 coffees, 2 donuts, 2 bagels, 1 fruit salad	13.50	
Drew	2 teas, 1 juice, 1 coffee, 3 muffins, 4 toasts	14.90	
Sharon	2 juices, 3 coffees, 1 bagel, 2 oatmeal, 2 fruit salads	23.25	✓
Veronica	3 teas, 2 coffees, 4 toasts, 1 fruit salad, 2 bagels, 1 muffin	17.35	✓
Mario	2 juices, 2 oatmeal, 2 fruit salads, 1 donut	17.75	✓
Debbie	4 coffees, 3 teas, 8 donuts, 1 bagel	16.60	
Jessica	1 juice, 1 oatmeal, 2 fruit salad, 2 muffins, 1 bagel	18.75	✓

5. Carly purchased 84 bulbs for her flower garden. Tulips came in trays containing six bulbs and daffodils came in trays containing 8 bulbs. Carly bought an equal number of tulip and daffodil trays. How many of each type of flower bulb were purchased?

Calculator Questions

1. If $\sqrt{1+x} = 4$, what is x?
   a. 10
   b. 15
   c. 20
   d. 25

2. What is the simplified quotient of the following equation?
$$\frac{5x^3}{3x^2y} \div \frac{25}{3y^9}$$

   a. $\frac{125x}{9y^{10}}$

   b. $\frac{x}{5y^8}$

   c. $\frac{5}{xy^8}$

   d. $\frac{xy^8}{5}$

3. Which of the following is a factor of both $x^2 + 4x + 4$ and $x^2 - x - 6$?
   a. $x - 3$
   b. $x + 2$
   c. $x - 2$
   d. $x + 3$

4. Which of the following shows the correct result of simplifying the following expression:
$$(7n + 3n^3 + 3) + (8n + 5n^3 + 2n^4)$$
   a. $9n^4 + 15n - 2$
   b. $2n^4 + 5n^3 + 15n - 2$
   c. $9n^4 + 8n^3 + 15n$
   d. $2n^4 + 8n^3 + 15n + 3$

5. Which of the following inequalities is equivalent to $3 - \frac{1}{2}x \geq 2$?
   a. $x \geq 2$
   b. $x \leq 2$
   c. $x \geq 1$
   d. $x \leq 1$

6. If $4x - 3 = 5$, then $x =$
   a. 1
   b. 2
   c. 3
   d. 4

7. What is the solution to the following system of equations?
$$x^2 - 2x + y = 8$$
$$x - y = -2$$
   a. $(-2, 3)$
   b. There is no solution.
   c. $(-2, 0)\ (1, 3)$
   d. $(-2, 0)\ (3, 5)$

8. A line passes through the point (1, 2) and crosses the y-axis at y = 1. Which of the following is an equation for this line?
   a. $y = 2x$
   b. $y = x + 1$
   c. $x + y = 1$
   d. $y = \frac{x}{2} - 2$

9. A company invests $50,000 in a building where they can produce saws. If the cost of producing one saw is $40, then which function expresses the amount of money the company pays? The variable y is the money paid and x is the number of saws produced.
   a. $y = 50{,}000x + 40$
   b. $y + 40 = x - 50{,}000$
   c. $y = 40x - 50{,}000$
   d. $y = 40x + 50{,}000$

10. If $g(x) = x^3 - 3x^2 - 2x + 6$ and $f(x) = 2$, then what is $g(f(x))$?
   a. -26
   b. 6
   c. $2x^3 - 6x^2 - 4x + 12$
   d. -2

11. Five students take a test. The scores of the first four students are 80, 85, 75, and 60. If the median score is 80, which of the following could NOT be the score of the fifth student?
   a. 60
   b. 80
   c. 85
   d. 100

12. What is the probability of randomly picking the winner and runner-up from a race of 4 horses and distinguishing which is the winner?
   a. $\frac{1}{4}$

   b. $\frac{1}{2}$

   c. $\frac{1}{16}$

   d. $\frac{1}{12}$

13. A grocery store is selling individual bottles of water, and each bottle contains 750 milliliters of water. If 12 bottles are purchased, what conversion will correctly determine how many liters that customer will take home?

    a. 100 milliliters equals 1 liter

    b. 1,000 milliliters equals 1 liter

    c. 1,000 liters equals 1 milliliter

    d. 10 liters equals 1 milliliter

14. Which of the following statements is true about the two lines below?

    a. The two lines are parallel but not perpendicular.

    b. The two lines are perpendicular but not parallel.

    c. The two lines are both parallel and perpendicular.

    d. The two lines are neither parallel nor perpendicular.

15. The perimeter of a 6-sided polygon is 56 cm. The length of three sides is 9 cm each. The length of two other sides is 8 cm each. What is the length of the missing side?

    a. 11 cm

    b. 12 cm

    c. 13 cm

    d. 10 cm

16. The area of a given rectangle is 24 centimeters. If the measure of each side is multiplied by 3, what is the area of the new figure?

    a. 48cm

    b. 72cm

    c. 216cm

    d. 13,824cm

17. Apples cost $2 each, while oranges cost $3 each. Maria purchased 10 fruits in total and spent $22. How many apples did she buy?

    a. 5

    b. 6

    c. 7

    d. 8

18. $(4x^2y^4)^{\frac{3}{2}}$ can be simplified to which of the following?

    a. $8x^3y^6$

    b. $4x^{\frac{5}{2}}y$

    c. $4xy$

    d. $32x^{\frac{7}{2}}y^{\frac{11}{2}}$

19. A line passes through the origin and through the point (-3, 4). What is the slope of the line?

   a. $-\frac{4}{3}$

   b. $-\frac{3}{4}$

   c. $\frac{4}{3}$

   d. $\frac{3}{4}$

20. $3\frac{2}{3} - 1\frac{4}{5} =$

   a. $1\frac{13}{15}$

   b. $\frac{14}{15}$

   c. $2\frac{2}{3}$

   d. $\frac{4}{5}$

21. Shawna buys $2\frac{1}{2}$ gallons of paint. If she uses $\frac{1}{3}$ of it on the first day, how much does she have left?

   a. $1\frac{5}{6}$ gallons

   b. $1\frac{1}{2}$ gallons

   c. $1\frac{2}{3}$ gallons

   d. 2 gallons

22. How will $\frac{4}{5}$ be written as a percent?

   a. 40%

   b. 125%

   c. 90%

   d. 80%

23. What are all the factors of 12?

   a. 12, 24, 36

   b. 1, 2, 4, 6, 12

   c. 12, 24, 36, 48

   d. 1, 2, 3, 4, 6, 12

24. At the beginning of the day, Xavier has 20 apples. At lunch, he meets his sister Emma and gives her half of his apples. After lunch, he stops by his neighbor Jim's house and gives him 6 of his apples. He then uses ¾ of his remaining apples to make an apple pie for dessert at dinner. At the end of the day, how many apples does Xavier have left?

   a. 4

   b. 6

   c. 2

   d. 1

25. How will the number 847.89632 be written if rounded to the nearest hundredth?
    a. 847.90
    b. 900
    c. 847.89
    d. 847.896

26. What is the value of the sum of $\frac{1}{3}$ and $\frac{2}{5}$?
    a. $\frac{3}{8}$

    b. $\frac{11}{15}$

    c. $\frac{11}{30}$

    d. $\frac{4}{5}$

27. Add and express in reduced form $5/12 + 4/9$.
    a. 9/17
    b. 1/3
    c. 31/36
    d. 3/5

28. Divide and reduce $4/13 \div 27/169$.
    a. 52/27
    b. 51/27
    c. 52/29
    d. 51/29

29. Express as a reduced mixed number 54/15.
    a. 3 3/5
    b. 3 1/15
    c. 3 3/54
    d. 3 1/54

30. In the problem $5 \times 6 + 4 \div 2 - 1$, which operation should be completed first?
    a. Multiplication
    b. Addition
    c. Division
    d. Subtraction

31. Express as an improper fraction 8 3/7.
    a. 11/7
    b. 21/8
    c. 5/3
    d. 59/7

32. When rounding 245.2678 to the nearest thousandth, which place value would be used to decide whether to round up or round down?
    a. Ten-thousandth
    b. Thousandth
    c. Hundredth
    d. Thousand

33. If $x > 3$, then $\dfrac{x^2-6x+9}{x^2-x-6} =$
    a. $\dfrac{x+2}{x-3}$
    b. $\dfrac{x-2}{x-3}$
    c. $\dfrac{x-3}{x+3}$
    d. $\dfrac{x-3}{x+2}$

34. If x is not zero, then $\dfrac{3}{x}+\dfrac{5u}{2x}-\dfrac{u}{4} =$
    a. $\dfrac{12+10u-ux}{4x}$

    b. $\dfrac{3+5u-ux}{x}$

    c. $\dfrac{12x+10u+ux}{4x}$

    d. $\dfrac{12+10u-u}{4x}$

35. If $4x - 3 = 5$, then $x =$
    a. 1
    b. 2
    c. 3
    d. 4

36. Solve for x, if $x^2 - 2x - 8 = 0$.
    a. $2 \pm \dfrac{\sqrt{30}}{2}$
    b. $2 \pm 4\sqrt{2}$
    c. 1 ± 3
    d. $4 \pm \sqrt{2}$

37. On Monday, Robert mopped the floor in 4 hours. On Tuesday, he did it in 3 hours. If on Monday, his average rate of mopping was p sq. ft. per hour, what was his average rate on Tuesday?
    a. $\dfrac{4}{3}p$ sq. ft. per hour

    b. $\dfrac{3}{4}p$ sq. ft. per hour

    c. $\dfrac{5}{4}p$ sq. ft. per hour

    d. $p + 1$ sq. ft. per hour

38. For which of the following are $x = 4$ and $x = -4$ solutions?
   a. $x^2 + 16 = 0$
   b. $x^2 + 4x - 4 = 0$
   c. $x^2 - 2x - 2 = 0$
   d. $x^2 - 16 = 0$

39. If $a \neq b$, solve for x if $\frac{1}{x} + \frac{2}{a} = \frac{2}{b}$
   a. $\frac{a-b}{ab}$

   b. $\frac{ab}{2(a-b)}$

   c. $\frac{2(a-b)}{ab}$

   d. $\frac{a-b}{2ab}$

40. If $x^2 + x - 3 = 0$, then $\left(x - \frac{1}{2}\right)^2 =$
   a. $\frac{11}{2}$

   b. $\frac{11}{4}$

   c. 11

   d. $\frac{121}{4}$

41. Which graph will be a line parallel to the graph of $y = 3x - 2$?
   a. $2y - 6x = 2$
   b. $y - 4x = 4$
   c. $3y = x - 2$
   d. $2x - 2y = 2$

42. Jessica buys 10 cans of paint. Red paint costs $1 per can and blue paint costs $2 per can. In total, she spends $16. How many red cans did she buy?
   a. 2
   b. 3
   c. 4
   d. 5

43. A farmer owns two (non-adjacent) square plots of land, which he wishes to fence. The area of one is 1000 square feet, while the area of the other is 10 square feet. How much fencing does he need, in feet?
   a. 44
   b. $40\sqrt{10}$
   c. $440\sqrt{10}$
   d. $44\sqrt{10}$

44. If $\log_{10} x = 2$, then x is
   a. 4
   b. 20
   c. 100
   d. 1000

45. $2x(3x + 1) - 5(3x + 1) =$
   a. $10x(3x + 1)$
   b. $10x^2(3x + 1)$
   c. $(2x - 5)(3x + 1)$
   d. $(2x + 1)(3x - 5)$

46. For which real numbers x is $-3x^2 + x - 8 > 0$?
   a. All real numbers x
   b. $-2\sqrt{\frac{2}{3}} < x < 2\sqrt{\frac{2}{3}}$
   c. $1 - 2\sqrt{\frac{2}{3}} < x < 1 + 2\sqrt{\frac{2}{3}}$
   d. For no real numbers x

47. A root of $x^2 - 2x - 2$ is
   a. $1 + \sqrt{3}$
   b. $1 + 2\sqrt{2}$
   c. $2 + 2\sqrt{3}$
   d. $2 - 2\sqrt{3}$

48. A line goes through the point (-4, 0) and the point (0,2). What is the slope of the line?
   a. 2
   b. 4
   c. $\frac{3}{2}$
   d. $\frac{1}{2}$

49. The sequence $\{a_n\}$ is defined by the relation $a_{n+1} = 3a_n - 1, a_1 = 1$. Find a_3.
   a. 2
   b. 4
   c. 5
   d. 15

50. What is the volume of a cube with the side equal to 3 inches?
   a. 6 in³
   b. 27 in³
   c. 9 in³
   d. 3 in³

51. What is the volume of a rectangular prism with a height of 2 inches, a width of 4 inches, and a depth of 6 inches?

    a. 12 in³

    b. 24 in³

    c. 48 in³

    d. 96 in³

52. What is the volume of a cylinder, in terms of π, with a radius of 5 inches and a height of 10 inches?

    a. 250 π in³

    b. 50 π in³

    c. 100 π in³

    d. 200 π in³

53. What is the volume of a pyramid, with the area of the base measuring 12 inches², and the height measuring 15 inches?

    a. 180 in³

    b. 90 in³

    c. 30 in³

    d. 60 in³

54. What is the volume of a sphere, in terms of π, with a radius of 3 inches?

    a. 36 π in³

    b. 27 π in³

    c. 9 π in³

    d. 72 π in³

55. What is the length of the hypotenuse of a right triangle with one leg equal to 3 centimeters and the other leg equal to 4 centimeters?

    a. 7 cm

    b. 5 cm

    c. 25 cm

    d. 12 cm

56. What is the answer to $(2 + 2i)(2 - 2i)$?

    a. 8

    b. 8i

    c. 4

    d. 4i

57. What is the answer to $\frac{2+2i}{2-2i}$?

    a. 8

    b. 8i

    c. 2i

    d. i

58. What is the length of an arc, in terms of π, that has an angle of 36° and a circle with a 10 centimeter radius?

    a. $\frac{\pi}{2}$ cm

    b. π cm

    c. 2π cm

    d. 4π cm

59. A builder is working with a mason and an architect to create part of a circle for a decorative roof. They need to know the length of the arc, in terms of π, that has an angle of 20° and a circle with a 108 centimeter radius?

    a. $10\,\pi$ cm

    b. $12\,\pi$ cm

    c. $20\,\pi$ cm

    d. $100\,\pi$ cm

60. What is the area of a circle, in terms of π, with a radius of 10 centimeters?

    a. $10\,\pi$ cm ^{2}

    b. $20\,\pi$ cm ^{2}

    c. $100\,\pi$ cm ^{2}

    d. $200\,\pi$ cm ^{2}

61. A landscaper is making a circular garden in his back yard, with a radius of 13 feet. He needs to compute the area to know how much soil to purchase. What is the area of the circle in terms of π?

    a. $26\,\pi$ ft ^{2}

    b. $169\,\pi$ ft ^{2}

    c. $130\,\pi$ ft ^{2}

    d. $260\,\pi$ ft ^{2}

Answer Explanations Test #1

1. C: The decimal points are lined up, with zeroes put in as needed. Then, the numbers are added just like integers:

$$
\begin{array}{r}
3.40 \\
2.35 \\
+4.00 \\
\hline
9.75
\end{array}
$$

1. D: The fraction is converted so that the denominator is 100 by multiplying the numerator and denominator by 4, to get $\frac{3}{25} = \frac{12}{100}$. Dividing a number by 100 just moves the decimal point two places to the left, with a result of 0.12.

2. B: 30% is 3/10. The number itself must be 10/3 of 6, or $\frac{10}{3} \times 6 = 10 \times 2 = 20$.

3. The completed scatter plot is below. Using the provided data table, one can determine that Cameron read 5 books in March and June, 4 books in August, and 1 book in September.

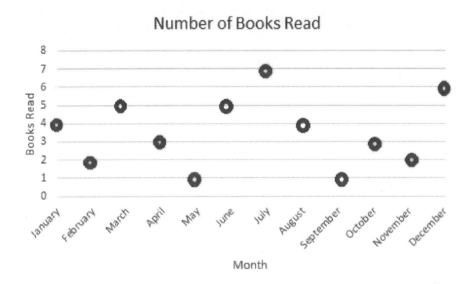

82

4. The following completed table shows the order totals and indicates which customers earned the free donut by exceeding $17.00.

Customer	Purchase	Total	Free Donut
Ben	4 coffees, 2 donuts, 2 bagels, 1 fruit salad	$14.50	
Drew	2 teas, 1 juice, 1 coffee, 3 muffins, 4 toasts	$14.90	
Sharon	2 juices, 3 coffees, 1 bagel, 2 oatmeal, 2 fruit salads	$23.25	✓
Veronica	3 teas, 2 coffees, 4 toasts, 1 fruit salad, 2 bagels, 1 muffin	$17.35	✓
Mario	2 juices, 2 oatmeal, 2 fruit salads, 1 donut	$17.75	✓
Debbie	4 coffees, 3 teas, 8 donuts, 1 bagel	$16.60	
Jessica	1 juice, 1 oatmeal, 2 fruit salad, 2 muffins, 1 bagel	$18.75	✓

5. 6: This problem involved setting up an algebraic equation to solve for x, or the number of flower trays Carly purchased. The equation is as follows:

$$6x + 8x = 84$$

So,

$$14x = 84$$

Then divide each side by 14 to solve for x:

$$x = \frac{84}{14} = 6 \; trays$$

Calculator Questions

1. B: Start by squaring both sides to get $1 + x = 16$. Then subtract 1 from both sides to get $x = 15$.

2. D: Dividing rational expressions follows the same rule as dividing fractions. The division is changed to multiplication, and the reciprocal is found in the second fraction. This turns the expression into $\frac{5x^3}{3x^2} * \frac{3y^9}{25}$. Multiplying across and simplifying, the final expression is $\frac{xy^8}{5}$.

3. B: To factor $x^2 + 4x + 4$, the numbers needed are those that add to 4 and multiply to 4. Therefore, both numbers must be 2, and the expression factors to $x^2 + 4x + 4 = (x + 2)^2$. Similarly, the expression factors to $x^2 - x - 6 = (x - 3)(x + 2)$, so that they have $x + 2$ in common.

4. D: The expression is simplified by collecting like terms. Terms with the same variable and exponent are like terms, and their coefficients can be added.

5. B: To simplify this inequality, subtract 3 from both sides to get $-\frac{1}{2}x \geq -1$. Then, multiply both sides by -2 (remembering this flips the direction of the inequality) to get $x \leq 2$.

6. B: Add 3 to both sides to get $4x = 8$. Then divide both sides by 4 to get $x = 2$.

7. D: This system of equations involves one quadratic function and one linear function, as seen from the degree of each equation. One way to solve this is through substitution. Solving for y in the second equation yields $y = x + 2$. Plugging this equation in for the y of the quadratic equation yields $x^2 - 2x + x + 2 = 8$. Simplifying the equation, it becomes $x^2 - x + 2 = 8$. Setting this equal to zero and factoring, it becomes $x^2 - x - 6 = 0 = (x - 3)(x + 2)$. Solving these two factors for x gives the zeros $x = 3, -2$. To find the y-value for the point, each number can be plugged in to either original equation. Solving each one for y yields the points $(3, 5)$ and $(-2, 0)$.

8. B: From the slope-intercept form, $y = mx + b$, it is known that b is the y-intercept, which is 1. Compute the slope as $\frac{2-1}{1-0} = 1$, so the equation should be $y = x + 1$.

9. D: For manufacturing costs, there is a linear relationship between the cost to the company and the number produced, with a y-intercept given by the base cost of acquiring the means of production, and a slope given by the cost to produce one unit. In this case, that base cost is $50,000, while the cost per unit is $40. So, $y = 40x + 50,000$.

10. D: This problem involves a composition function, where one function is plugged into the other function. In this case, the $f(x)$ function is plugged into the $g(x)$ function for each x-value. The composition equation becomes $g(f(x)) = 2^3 - 3(2^2) - 2(2) + 6$. Simplifying the equation gives the answer $g(f(x)) = 8 - 3(4) - 2(2) + 6 = 8 - 12 - 4 + 6 = -2$.

11. A: Lining up the given scores provides the following list: 60, 75, 80, 85, and one unknown. Because the median needs to be 80, it means 80 must be the middle data point out of these five. Therefore, the unknown data point must be the fourth or fifth data point, meaning it must be greater than or equal to 80. The only answer that fails to meet this condition is 60.

12. D: $\frac{1}{12}$. The probability of picking the winner of the race is $\frac{1}{4}$ $\left(\frac{number\ of\ favorable\ outcomes}{number\ of\ total\ outcomes}\right)$. Assuming the winner was picked on the first selection, three horses remain from which to choose the runner-up (these are dependent events). Therefore, the probability of picking the runner-up is $\frac{1}{3}$. To determine the probability of multiple events, the probability of each event is multiplied: $\frac{1}{4} \times \frac{1}{3} = \frac{1}{12}$.

13. B: $12 \times 750 = 9,000$. Therefore, there are 9,000 milliliters of water, which must be converted to liters. 1,000 milliliters equals 1 liter; therefore, 9 liters of water are purchased.

14. D: The two lines are neither parallel nor perpendicular. Parallel lines will never intersect or meet. Therefore, the lines are not parallel. Perpendicular lines intersect to form a right angle (90°). Although the lines intersect, they do not form a right angle, which is usually indicated with a box at the intersection point. Therefore, the lines are not perpendicular.

15. C: Perimeter is found by calculating the sum of all sides of the polygon. $9 + 9 + 9 + 8 + 8 + s = 56$, where s is the missing side length. Therefore, 43 plus the missing side length is equal to 56. The missing side length is 13 cm.

16. C: 216cm. Because area is a two-dimensional measurement, the dimensions are multiplied by a scale that is squared to determine the scale of the corresponding areas. The dimensions of the rectangle are multiplied by a scale of 3. Therefore, the area is multiplied by a scale of 3^2 (which is equal to 9): $24cm \times 9 = 216cm$.

17. D: Let a be the number of apples and o the number of oranges. Then, the total cost is $2a + 3o = 22$, while it also known that $a + o = 10$. Using the knowledge of systems of equations, cancel the o variables by multiplying the second equation by -3. This makes the equation $-3a - 3o = -30$. Adding this to the first equation, the o values cancel to get $-a = -8$, which simplifies to $a = 8$.

18. A: Simplify this to $(4x^2y^4)^{\frac{3}{2}} = 4^{\frac{3}{2}}(x^2)^{\frac{3}{2}}(y^4)^{\frac{3}{2}}$. Now, $4^{\frac{3}{2}} = (\sqrt{4})^3 = 2^3 = 8$. For the other, recall that the exponents must be multiplied, so this yields $8x^{2\cdot\frac{3}{2}}y^{4\cdot\frac{3}{2}} = 8x^3y^6$.

19. A: The slope is given by $m = \frac{y_2 - y_1}{x_2 - x_1} = \frac{0 - 4}{0 - (-3)} = -\frac{4}{3}$.

20. A: These numbers to improper fractions: $\frac{11}{3} - \frac{9}{5}$. Take 15 as a common denominator: $\frac{11}{3} - \frac{9}{5} = : \frac{55}{15} - \frac{27}{15} = \frac{28}{15} = 1\frac{13}{15}$ (when rewritten to get rid of the partial fraction).

21. C: If she has used 1/3 of the paint, she has 2/3 remaining. $2\frac{1}{2}$ gallons are the same as $\frac{5}{2}$ gallons. The calculation is $\frac{2}{3} \times \frac{5}{2} = \frac{5}{3} = 1\frac{2}{3}$ gallons.

22. D: 80%. To convert a fraction to a percent, the fraction is first converted to a decimal. To do so, the numerator is divided by the denominator: $4 \div 5 = 0.8$. To convert a decimal to a percent, the number is multiplied by 100: $0.8 \times 100 = 80\%$.

23. D: 1, 2, 3, 4, 6, 12. A given number divides evenly by each of its factors to produce an integer (no decimals). The number 5, 7, 8, 9, 10, 11 (and their opposites) do not divide evenly into 12. Therefore, these numbers are not factors.

24. D: This problem can be solved using basic arithmetic. Xavier starts with 20 apples, then gives his sister half, so 20 divided by 2.

$$\frac{20}{2} = 10$$

He then gives his neighbor 6, so 6 is subtracted from 10.

$$10 - 6 = 4$$

Lastly, he uses ¾ of his apples to make an apple pie, so to find remaining apples, the first step is to subtract ¾ from one and then multiply the difference by 4.

$$\left(1 - \frac{3}{4}\right) \times 4 = ?$$

$$\left(\frac{4}{4} - \frac{3}{4}\right) \times 4 = ?$$

$$\left(\frac{1}{4}\right) \times 4 = 1$$

25. A: 847.90. The hundredth place value is located two digits to the right of the decimal point (the digit 9). The digit to the right of the place value is examined to decide whether to round up or keep the digit. In this case, the digit 6 is 5 or greater so the hundredth place is rounded up. When rounding up, if the digit to be increased is a 9, the digit to its left is increased by one and the digit in the desired place value is made a zero. Therefore, the number is rounded to 847.90.

26. B: $\frac{11}{15}$. Fractions must have like denominators to be added. The least common multiple of the denominators 3 and 5 is found. The LCM is 15, so both fractions should be changed to equivalent fractions with a denominator of 15. To determine the numerator of the new fraction, the old numerator is multiplied by the same number by which the old denominator is multiplied to obtain the new denominator. For the fraction $\frac{1}{3}$, 3 multiplied by 5 will produce 15. Therefore, the numerator is multiplied by 5 to produce the new numerator $\left(\frac{1\times5}{3\times5} = \frac{5}{15}\right)$. For the fraction $\frac{2}{5}$, multiplying both the numerator and denominator by 3 produces $\frac{6}{15}$. When fractions have like denominators, they are added by adding the numerators and keeping the denominator the same: $\frac{5}{15} + \frac{6}{15} = \frac{11}{15}$.

27. C: 31/36

Set up the problem and find a common denominator for both fractions.

$$\frac{5}{12} + \frac{4}{9}$$

Multiply each fraction across by 1 to convert to a common denominator.

$$\frac{5}{12} \times \frac{3}{3} + \frac{4}{9} \times \frac{4}{4}$$

Once over the same denominator, add across the top. The total is over the common denominator.

$$\frac{15 + 16}{36} = \frac{31}{36}$$

28. A: 52/27

Set up the division problem.

$$\frac{4}{13} \div \frac{27}{169}$$

Flip the second fraction and multiply.

$$\frac{4}{13} \times \frac{169}{27}$$

Simplify and reduce with cross multiplication.

$$\frac{4}{1} \times \frac{13}{27}$$

Multiply across the top and across the bottom to solve.

$$\frac{4 \times 13}{1 \times 27} = \frac{52}{27}$$

29. A: 3 3/5

Divide.

$$15 \overline{)54} \;\; 3$$

$$\begin{array}{r} 3 \\ 15{\overline{)54}} \\ -45 \\ \hline 9 \end{array}$$

The result is 3 9/15.

Reduce the remainder for the final answer.

3 3/5

30. A: Using the order of operations, multiplication and division are computed first from left to right. Multiplication is on the left; therefore, the teacher should perform multiplication first.

31. D: 59/7

The original number was 8 3/7. Multiply the denominator by the whole number portion. Add the numerator and put the total over the original denominator.

$$\frac{(8 \times 7) + 3}{7} = \frac{59}{7}$$

32. A: The place value to the right of the thousandth place, which would be the ten-thousandth place, is what gets used. The value in the thousandth place is 7. The number in the place value to its right is greater than 4, so the 7 gets bumped up to 8. Everything to its right turns to a zero, to get 245.2680. The zero is dropped because it is part of the decimal.

33. D: Factor the numerator into $x^2 - 6x + 9 = (x - 3)^2$, since $-3 - 3 = -6, (-3)(-3) = 9$. Factor the denominator into $x^2 - x - 6 = (x - 3)(x + 2)$, since $-3 + 2 = -1, (-3)(2) = -6$. This means the rational function can be rewritten as $\frac{x^2-6x+9}{x^2-x-6} = \frac{(x-3)^2}{(x-3)(x+2)}$. Using the restriction of x > 3, do not worry about any of these terms being 0, and cancel an $x - 3$ from the numerator and the denominator, leaving $\frac{x-3}{x+2}$.

34. C: The common denominator here will be 4x. Rewrite these fractions as $\frac{3}{x} + \frac{5u}{2x} - \frac{u}{4} = \frac{12}{4x} + \frac{10u}{4x} - \frac{ux}{4x} = \frac{12x+10u+ux}{4x}$.

35. B: Add 3 to both sides to get $4x = 8$. Then divide both sides by 4 to get $x = 2$.

36. C: The numbers needed are those that add to -2 and multiply to -8. The difference between 2 and 4 is 2. Their product is 8, and -4 and 2 will work. Therefore, $x^2 - 2x - 8 = (x - 4)(x + 2)$. The latter has roots 4 and -2 or 1 ± 3.

37. A: Robert accomplished his task on Tuesday in ¾ the time compared to Monday. He must have worked 4/3 as fast.

38. D: There are two ways to approach this problem. Each value can be substituted into each equation. A can be eliminated, since $4^2 + 16 = 32$. Choice B can be eliminated, since $4^2 + 4 \cdot 4 - 4 = 28$. C can be eliminated, since $4^2 - 2 \cdot 4 - 2 = 6$. But, plugging in either value into $x^2 - 16$, which gives $(\pm 4)^2 - 16 = 16 - 16 = 0$.

39. B: $\frac{2}{a}$ must be subtracted from both sides, with a result of $\frac{1}{x} = \frac{2}{b} - \frac{2}{a}$. The reciprocal of both sides needs to be taken, but the right-hand side needs to be written as a single fraction in order to do that. Since the two fractions on the right have denominators that are not equal, a common denominator of ab is needed. This leaves $\frac{1}{x} = \frac{2a}{ab} - \frac{2b}{ab} = \frac{2(a-b)}{ab}$. Taking the reciprocals, which can be done since $b - a$ is not zero, with a result of $x = \frac{ab}{2(a-b)}$.

40. B: Plugging into the quadratic formula yields, for solutions $x = \frac{1 \pm \sqrt{-1 + 4 \cdot 1 \cdot (-3)}}{2} = \frac{1}{2} \pm \frac{\sqrt{11}}{2}$. Therefore, $x - \frac{1}{2} = \pm \frac{\sqrt{11}}{2}$. Now, if this is squared, then the $\pm$ cancels and left with $\left(\frac{\sqrt{11}}{2}\right)^2 = \frac{11}{4}$.

41. A: Parallel lines have the same slope. The slope of C can be seen to be 1/3 by dividing both sides by 3. For E, divide both sides by 2 and see the slope is 3/2. The others are in standard form $Ax + By = C$, for which the slope is given by $\frac{-A}{B}$. The slope of A is 3, the slope of B is 4. The slope of D is 1.

42. C: Let r be the number of red cans and b be the number of blue cans. One equation is $r + b = 10$. The total price is \$16, and the prices for each can means $1r + 2b = 16$. Multiplying the first equation on both sides by -1 results in $-r - b = -10$. Add this equation to the second equation, leaving $b = 6$. So, she bought 6 *blue* cans. From the first equation, this means $r = 4$; thus, she bought 4 *red* cans.

43. D: The first field has an area of 1000 feet, so the length of one side is $\sqrt{1000} = 10\sqrt{10}$. Since there are four sides to a square, the total perimeter is $40\sqrt{10}$. The second square has an area of 10 square feet, so the length of one side is $\sqrt{10}$, and the total perimeter is $4\sqrt{10}$. Adding these together gives $40\sqrt{10} + 4\sqrt{10} = (40 + 4)\sqrt{10} = 44\sqrt{10}$.

44. C: If $\log_{10} x = 2$, then $10^2 = x$, which equals 100.

45. C: The $(3x + 1)$ can be factored to get $(2x - 5)(3x + 1)$.

46. D: Because the coefficient of x^2 is negative, this function has a graph that is a parabola that opens downward. Therefore, it will be greater than 0 between its real roots, if it has any. Checking the discriminant, the result is $1^2 - 4(-3)(-8) = 1 - 96 = -95$. Since the discriminant is negative, this equation has no real solutions. Since this has no real roots, it must be always positive or always negative. Its graph opens downward, so it has at least some negative values. That means it is always negative. Thus, it is bigger than zero for no real numbers.

47. A: Check each value, but it is easiest to use the quadratic formula, which gives $x = \frac{2 \pm \sqrt{(-2)^2 - 4(1)(-2)}}{2} = 1 \pm \frac{\sqrt{12}}{2} = 1 \pm \frac{2\sqrt{3}}{2} = 1 \pm \sqrt{3}$. The only one of these which appears as an answer choice is $1 + \sqrt{3}$.

48. D: The slope is given by the change in y divided by the change in x. The change in y is 2-0 = 2, and the change in x is $0 - (-4) = 4$. The slope is $\frac{2}{4} = \frac{1}{2}$.

49. C: Find $a_2 = 3a_1 - 1 = 3 \cdot 1 - 1 = 2$. Next, find $a_3 = 3a_2 - 1 = 3 \cdot 2 - 1 = 5$.

50. B: The volume of a cube is the length of the side cubed, and 3 inches cubed is 27 in³. Choice *A* is not the correct answer because that is 2×3 inches. Choice *C* is not the correct answer because that is 3×3 inches, and Choice *D* is not the correct answer because there was no operation performed.

51. C: The volume of a rectangular prism is $length \times width \times height$, and $2\ inches \times 4\ inches \times 6\ inches\ is\ 48\ in^3$. Choice *A* is not the correct answer because that is $2\ inches \times 6\ inches$. Choice *B* is not the correct answer because that is $4\ inches \times 6\ inches$. Choice *D* is not the correct answer because that is double of all the sides multiplied together.

52. A: The volume of a cylinder is $\pi r^2 h$, and $\pi \times 5^2 \times 10$ is $250\ \pi\ in^3$. Choice *B* is not the correct answer because that is $5^2 \times 2\pi$. Choice *C* is not the correct answer since that is $5cm \times 10\pi$. Choice *D* is not the correct answer because that is $10^2 \times 2cm$.

53. D: The volume of a pyramid is $(length \times width \times height)$, divided by 3, and (12×15), divided by 3 is 60 in³. Choice *A* is not the correct answer because that is 12×15. Choice *B* is not the correct answer because that is (12×15), divided by 2. Choice *C* is not the correct answer because that is 15×2.

54. A: The formula for the volume of a sphere is $\frac{4}{3}\pi r^3$, and $\frac{4}{3} \times \pi \times 3^3$ is $36\ \pi\ in^3$. Choice *B* is not the correct answer because that is only 3^3. Choice *C* is not the correct answer because that is 3^2, and Choice *D* is not the correct answer because that is 36×2.

55. B: This answer is correct because $3^2 + 4^2$ is $9 + 16$, which is 25. Taking the square root of 25 is 5. Choice *A* is not the correct answer because that is $3 + 4$. Choice *C* is not the correct answer because that is stopping at $3^2 + 4^2$ is $9 + 16$, which is 25. Choice *D* is not the correct answer because that is 3×4.

56. A: This answer is correct because $(2 + 2i)(2 - 2i)$, using the FOIL method is: $4 - 4i + 4i - 4i^2 = 8$. Choice *B* is not the answer because there is no *i* in the final answer, since the *i*'s cancel out in the FOIL. Choice *C*, 4, is not the final answer because we add $4 + 4$ in the end to equal 8. Choice *D*, 4*i*, is not the final answer because there is neither a 4 nor an *i* in the final answer.

57. D: Multiply the top and the bottom by $(2 + 2i)$, the conjugate, to arrive at $\frac{8i}{8}$, which cancels to *i*. Choice *A* is not the answer because the 8's cancel out. Choice *B* is not the answer because the 8's cancel out. Choice *C* is not the answer because 2 is not left, but 8 is.

58. C: The formula for the length of an arc is $(central\ angle) \times (2\pi r) = (arc\ length) \times (360°)$, and $(36°)(2\pi 10) = (arc\ length) \times (360°)$, which reduces to 2π centimeters. Choice *A* is not the answer because the 2 is in the denominator. Choice *B* is not the answer since it was not multiplied by 2. Choice *D* is not the answer because it is double the correct arc length.

59. B: The formula for the length of an arc is $(central\ angle) \times (2\pi r) = (arc\ length) \times (360°)$ and $(20°)(2\pi 108) = (arc\ length) \times (360°)$. Choices *A*, *C*, and *D*, are not correct because they signify that the simplification was performed incorrectly.

60. C: The formula for the area of the circle is πr^2 and 10^2 is 100. Choice *A* is not the correct answer because 10 is not squared. Choice *B* is not the correct answer because that is 2×10. Choice *D* is not the correct answer because that is $r^2 \times 2$.

61. B: The formula for the area of the circle is πr^2 and 13 squared is 169. Choice *A* is not the correct answer because that is 13×2. Choice *C* is not the correct answer because that is 13×10. Choice *D* is not the correct answer because that is $2 \times 13 \times 10$.

Practice Test #2

No Calculator Questions

1. $\frac{3}{25} =$
   a. 0.15
   b. 0.1
   c. 0.9
   d. 0.12

2. What is the value of the following expression?

$$\sqrt{8^2 + 6^2}$$

   a. 14
   b. 10
   c. 9
   d. 100

3. $864 \div 36 =$
   a. 24
   b. 25
   c. 34
   d. 18

4. Ms. Temple's fifth grade class has received some grades for the geometry math unit. Each student who achieves at least an 80% overall average on the three graded criteria will receive a star. Each score is weighted equally so they all contribute equally toward the overall average. Using the scores for the quiz, homework, and participation for each student, determine which students have met the 80% minimum and place a star in the appropriate box.

Name	Quiz Score	Homework Score	Participation	Star
Brian	8/10	2/5	9/10	
Kelsey	6/10	4/5	8/10	
Brad	7/10	4/5	9/10	
Xavier	9/10	3/5	9/10	
Julie	10/10	3/5	9/10	
Taylor	5/10	4/5	10/10	
Paulina	6/10	5/5	8/10	
Mario	8/10	1/5	7/10	

5. A pizzeria owner regularly creates jumbo pizzas, each with a radius of 9 inches. She is mathematically inclined, and wants to know the area of the pizza to purchase the correct boxes and know how much she is feeding her customers. What is the area of the circle, in terms of π, with a radius of 9 inches?

_____

Calculator Questions

1. $5.88 \times 3.2 =$
    a. 18.816
    b. 16.44
    c. 20.352
    d. 17

2. How will the following number be written in standard form: $(1 \times 10^4) + (3 \times 10^3) + (7 \times 10^1) + (8 \times 10^0)$
    a. 137
    b. 13,078
    c. 1,378
    d. 8,731

3. What is the value of the expression: $7^2 - 3 \times (4 + 2) + 15 \div 5$?
    a. 12.2
    b. 40.2
    c. 34
    d. 58.2

4. Four people split a bill. The first person pays for $\frac{1}{5}$, the second person pays for $\frac{1}{4}$, and the third person pays for $\frac{1}{3}$. What fraction of the bill does the fourth person pay?
    a. $\frac{13}{60}$
    b. $\frac{47}{60}$
    c. $\frac{1}{4}$
    d. $\frac{4}{15}$

5. A student gets an 85% on a test with 20 questions. How many answers did the student solve correctly?
    a. 15
    b. 16
    c. 17
    d. 18

6. What is $\frac{420}{98}$ rounded to the nearest integer?
    a. 4
    b. 3
    c. 5
    d. 6

7. If Danny takes 48 minutes to walk 3 miles, how long should it take him to walk 5 miles maintaining the same speed?

    a. 32 min

    b. 64 min

    c. 80 min

    d. 96 min

8. Is the following function even, odd, neither, or both?

$$y = \frac{1}{2}x^4 + 2x^2 - 6$$

    a. Even

    b. Odd

    c. Neither

    d. Both

9. An investment of $2,000 is made into an account with an annual interest rate of 5%, compounded continuously. What is the total value for the investment after eight years?

    a. $4,707

    b. $3,000

    c. $2,983.65

    d. $10, 919.63

10. What is the 42nd item in the pattern: ▲○○□ ▲○○□ ▲ …?

    a. ○

    b. ▲

    c. □

    d. None of the above

11. For a group of 20 men, the median weight is 180 pounds and the range is 30 pounds. If each man gains 10 pounds, which of the following would be true?

    a. The median weight will increase, and the range will remain the same.

    b. The median weight and range will both remain the same.

    c. The median weight will stay the same, and the range will increase.

    d. The median weight and range will both increase.

12. Ten students take a test. Five students get a 50. Four students get a 70. If the average score is 55, what was the last student's score?

    a. 20

    b. 40

    c. 50

    d. 60

13. Given the value of a given stock at monthly intervals, which graph should be used to best represent the trend of the stock?

    a. Box plot

    b. Line plot

    c. Line graph

    d. Circle graph

14. A six-sided die is rolled. What is the probability that the roll is 1 or 2?

    a. $\frac{1}{6}$

    b. $\frac{1}{4}$

    c. $\frac{1}{3}$

    d. $\frac{1}{2}$

15. An equilateral triangle has a perimeter of 18 feet. If a square whose sides have the same length as one side of the triangle is built, what will be the area of the square?

    a. 6 square feet

    b. 36 square feet

    c. 256 square feet

    d. 1000 square feet

16. What is the value of $x^2 - 2xy + 2y^2$ when $x = 2, y = 3$?

    a. 8

    b. 10

    c. 12

    d. 14

17. The square and circle have the same center. The circle has a radius of r. What is the area of the shaded region?

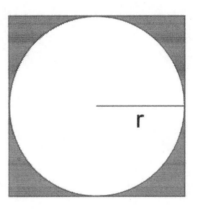

    a. $r^2 - \pi r^2$

    b. $4r^2 - 2\pi r$

    c. $(4 - \pi)r^2$

    d. $(\pi - 1)r^2$

18. What is the expression that represents three times the sum of twice a number and one minus 6?

    a. $2x + 1 - 6$

    b. $3x + 1 - 6$

    c. $3(x + 1) - 6$

    d. $3(2x + 1) - 6$

19. What are the coordinates of the two points marked with green dots on this coordinate plane?

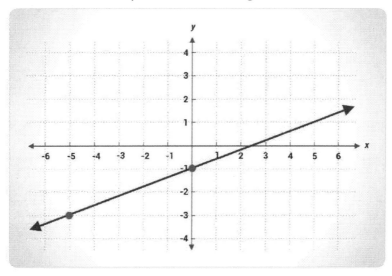

    a. (-3, -5) and (-1, 0)
    b. (5, 3) and (0, 1)
    c. (-5, -3) and (0, -1)
    d. (-3, -5) and (0, -1)

20. What is the value of x for the right triangle shown below?

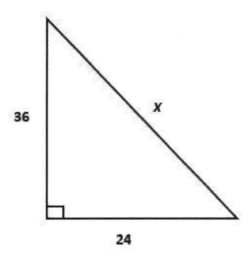

    a. 43.3
    b. 26.8
    c. 42.7
    d. 44.1

21. A cube has sides that are 7 inches long. What is the cube's volume?
    a. $49in^3$
    b. $343in^3$
    c. $294in^3$
    d. $28in^3$

22. Which of the following is largest?
   a. 0.45
   b. 0.096
   c. 0.3
   d. 0.313

23. Which of the following is NOT a way to write 40 percent of *N*?
   a. $(0.4)N$
   b. $\frac{2}{5}N$
   c. $40N$
   d. $\frac{4N}{10}$

24. Which is closest to 17.8×9.9?
   a. 140
   b. 180
   c. 200
   d. 350

25. $3\frac{2}{3} - 1\frac{4}{5} =$
   a. $1\frac{13}{15}$
   b. $\frac{14}{15}$
   c. $2\frac{2}{3}$
   d. $\frac{4}{5}$

26. $4\frac{1}{3} + 3\frac{3}{4} =$
   a. $6\frac{5}{12}$
   b. $8\frac{1}{12}$
   c. $8\frac{2}{3}$
   d. $7\frac{7}{12}$

27. Five of six numbers have a sum of 25. The average of all six numbers is 6. What is the sixth number?
   a. 8
   b. 10
   c. 11
   d. 12

28. $52.3 \times 10^{-3} =$
   a. 0.00523
   b. 0.0523
   c. 0.523
   d. 523

29. If $\frac{5}{2} \div \frac{1}{3} = n$, then n is between:
    a. 5 and 7
    b. 7 and 9
    c. 9 and 11
    d. 3 and 5

30. A closet is filled with red, blue, and green shirts. If $\frac{1}{3}$ of the shirts are green and $\frac{2}{5}$ are red, what fraction of the shirts are blue?
    a. $\frac{4}{15}$
    b. $\frac{1}{5}$
    c. $\frac{7}{15}$
    d. $\frac{1}{2}$

31. Express as an improper fraction 11 5/8.
    a. 55/8
    b. 93/8
    c. 16/11
    d. 19/5

32. Round to the nearest tenth 8.067.
    a. 8.07
    b. 8.10
    c. 8.00
    d. 8.11

33. Which of the following is the result of simplifying the expression:

$$\frac{4a^{-1}b^3}{a^4b^{-2}} * \frac{3a}{b}$$

    a. $12a^3b^5$

    b. $12\frac{b^4}{a^4}$

    c. $\frac{12}{a^4}$

    d. $7\frac{b^4}{a}$

34. The graph shows the position of a car over a 6-second time interval. Which of the following is the correct interpretation of the graph for the interval 1 to 3 seconds?

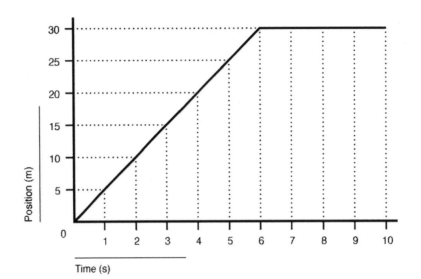

a. The car remains in the same position.
b. The car is traveling at a speed of 20m/s.
c. The car is traveling up a hill.
d. The car is traveling at 20mph.

35. What is the product of the following expression?

$$(4x - 8)(5x^2 + x + 6)$$

a. $20x^3 - 36x^2 + 16x - 48$
b. $6x^3 - 41x^2 + 12x + 15$
c. $204 + 11x^2 - 37x - 12$
d. $2x^3 - 11x^2 - 32x + 20$

36. What is the solution for the following equation?

$$\frac{x^2 + x - 30}{x - 5} = 11$$

a. $x = -6$
b. There is no solution.
c. $x = 16$
d. $x = 5$

37. What is the value of $x^2 - 2xy + 2y^2$ when $x = 2, y = 3$?
a. 8
b. 10
c. 12
d. 14

38. If $x > 3$, then $\frac{x^2-6x+9}{x^2-x-6} =$

    a. $\frac{x+2}{x-3}$

    b. $\frac{x-2}{x-3}$

    c. $\frac{x-3}{x+3}$

    d. $\frac{x-3}{x+2}$

39. What are the y-intercept(s) for $y = x^2 + 3x - 4$?

    a. $y = 1$

    b. $y = -4$

    c. $y = 3$

    d. $y = 4$

40. Which equation is not a function?

    a. $y = |x|$

    b. $y = \sqrt{x}$

    c. $x = 3$

    d. $y = 4$

41. What is the answer to $(2 + 2i)(2 - 2i)$?

    a. 8

    b. 8i

    c. 4

    d. 4i

42. What is the answer to $\frac{2+2i}{2-2i}$?

    a. 8

    b. 8i

    c. 2i

    d. i

43. Write the expression for three times the sum of twice a number and one minus 6.

    a. $2x + 1 - 6$

    b. $3x + 1 - 6$

    c. $3(x + 1) - 6$

    d. $3(2x + 1) - 6$

44. For which of the following are $x = 4$ and $x = -4$ solutions?

    a. $x^2 + 16 = 0$

    b. $x^2 + 4x - 4 = 0$

    c. $x^2 - 2x - 2 = 0$

    d. $x^2 - 16 = 0$

45. Which graph will be a line parallel to the graph of $y = 3x - 2$?

    a. $2y - 6x = 2$

    b. $y - 4x = 4$

    c. $3y = x - 2$

    d. $2x - 2y = 2$

46. An equation for the line passing through the origin and the point $(2, 1)$ is
   a. $y = 2x$
   b. $y = \frac{1}{2}x$
   c. $y = x - 2$
   d. $2y = x + 1$

47. A farmer owns two (non-adjacent) square plots of land, which he wishes to fence. The area of one is 1000 square feet, while the area of the other is 10 square feet. How much fencing does he need, in feet?
   a. 44
   b. $40\sqrt{10}$
   c. $440\sqrt{10}$
   d. $44\sqrt{10}$

48. If $\log_{10} x = 2$, then x is
   a. 4
   b. 20
   c. 100
   d. 1000

49. $2x(3x + 1) - 5(3x + 1) =$
   a. $10x(3x + 1)$
   b. $10x^2(3x + 1)$
   c. $(2x - 5)(3x + 1)$
   d. $(2x + 1)(3x - 5)$

50. For which real numbers x is $-3x^2 + x - 8 > 0$?
   a. All real numbers x
   b. $-2\sqrt{\frac{2}{3}} < x < 2\sqrt{\frac{2}{3}}$
   c. $1 - 2\sqrt{\frac{2}{3}} < x < 1 + 2\sqrt{\frac{2}{3}}$
   d. For no real numbers x

51. How many different ways can we order the letters a, b, c?
   a. 3
   b. 6
   c. 9
   d. 12

52. Six people apply to work for Janice's company, but she only needs four workers. How many different groups of four employees can Janice choose?
   a. 6
   b. 10
   c. 15
   d. 36

53. What is the volume of a cube with the side equal to 5 centimeters?
   a. 10 cm³
   b. 15 cm³
   c. 50 cm³
   d. 125 cm³

54. What is the volume of a rectangular prism with the height of 3 centimeters, a width of 5 centimeters, and a depth of 11 centimeters?
   a. 19 cm³
   b. 165 cm³
   c. 225 cm³
   d. 150 cm³

55. What is the volume of a cylinder, in terms of π, with a radius of 6 centimeters and a height of 2 centimeters?
   a. 36 π cm³
   b. 24 π cm³
   c. 72 π cm³
   d. 48 π cm³

56. What is the volume of a pyramid, with a square base whose side is 6 inches, and the height is 9 inches?
   a. 324 in³
   b. 72 in³
   c. 108 in³
   d. 18 in³

57. What is the volume of a sphere, in terms of π, with a radius of 6 centimeters?
   a. 144 π cm³
   b. 200 π cm³
   c. 288 π cm³
   d. 120 π cm³

58. What is the length of the other leg of a right triangle with a hypotenuse of 10 inches and a leg of 8 inches?
   a. 6 in
   b. 18 in
   c. 80 in
   d. 13 in

59. What is the answer to $(3 + 3i)(3 - 3i)$?
   a. 18
   b. 18i
   c. 9
   d. 9i

60. What is the answer to $\frac{3+3i}{3-3i}$?

    a. 18

    b. 18*i*

    c. *i*

    d. 9*i*

61. What is the length of the arc, in terms of π, that has an angle of 72° and a circle with a 20 inch radius?

    a. 8 π in

    b. 4 π in

    c. 2 π in

    d. π in

62. What is the area of a circle, in terms of π, with a radius of 5 centimeters?

    a. 10 π cm ^{2}

    b. 15 π cm ^{2}

    c. 20 π cm ^{2}

    d. 25 π cm ^{2}

Answer Explanations Test #2

No Calculator Questions

1. D: The fraction is converted so that the denominator is 100 by multiplying the numerator and denominator by 4, to get $\frac{3}{25} = \frac{12}{100}$. Dividing a number by 100 just moves the decimal point two places to the left, with a result of 0.12.

2. B: 8 squared is 64, and 6 squared is 36. These should be added together to get $64 + 36 = 100$. Then, the last step is to find the square root of 100 which is 10.

3. A: The long division would be completed as follows:

$$
\begin{array}{r}
24 \\
36\overline{)864} \\
-72\downarrow \\
\hline
144
\end{array}
$$

4. The table below shows the students who achieved at least an 80% average and earned a star.

Name	Quiz Score	Homework Score	Participation	Star
Brian	8/10	2/5	9/10	
Kelsey	6/10	4/5	8/10	
Brad	7/10	4/5	9/10	☆
Xavier	9/10	3/5	9/10	☆
Julie	10/10	3/5	9/10	☆
Taylor	5/10	4/5	10/10	
Paulina	6/10	5/5	8/10	☆
Mario	8/10	1/5	7/10	

This problem involved summing the three fractional scores for each student and then converting that total to a percentage. The quiz and participation scores were conveniently presented as fractions out of ten, but in order to add the homework score, which is out of five, a common denominator (of 10) needed to be use. This simply involved multiplying both the numerator and denominator of the homework score by 2. Because a cutoff of 80% was all that was needed to earn a star, it is actually not necessary to convert every student's score to a percentage. The minimum summed fraction that equals 80% can be found and then scores could be compared to that value. After converting the homework scores to fractions out of ten, each student's score will be some number out of 30. The fraction out of 30 that is equivalent to 80 percent is 24:

$$\frac{x}{30} = \frac{80}{100}$$

Cross-multiplying finds that $100x = 2400, x = 24$.

Therefore, each student must achieve at least 24 points out of the possible 30 to get the star.

5. 81π: The formula for the area of the circle is πr^2 and 9 squared is 81.

Calculator Questions

1. A: This problem can be multiplied as 588×32, except at the end, the decimal point needs to be moved three places to the left. Performing the multiplication will give 18,816, and moving the decimal place over three places results in 18.816.

2. B: 13,078. The power of 10 by which a digit is multiplied corresponds with the number of zeros following the digit when expressing its value in standard form. Therefore, $(1 \times 10^4) + (3 \times 10^3) + (7 \times 10^1) + (8 \times 10^0) = 10,000 + 3,000 + 70 + 8 = 13,078$.

3. C: 34. When performing calculations consisting of more than one operation, the order of operations should be followed: Parenthesis, Exponents, Multiplication/Division, Addition/Subtraction. Parenthesis: $7^2 - 3 \times (4 + 2) + 15 \div 5 = 7^2 - 3 \times (6) + 15 \div 5$. Exponents: $7^2 - 3 \times 6 + 15 \div 5 = 49 - 3 \times 6 + 15 \div 5$. Multiplication/Division (from left to right): $49 - 3 \times 6 + 15 \div 5 = 49 - 18 + 3$. Addition/Subtraction (from left to right): $49 - 18 + 3 = 34$.

4. A: To find the fraction of the bill that the first three people pay, the fractions need to be added, which means finding common denominator. The common denominator will be 60. $\frac{1}{5} + \frac{1}{4} + \frac{1}{3} = \frac{12}{60} + \frac{15}{60} + \frac{20}{60} = \frac{47}{60}$. The remainder of the bill is $1 - \frac{47}{60} = \frac{60}{60} - \frac{47}{60} = \frac{13}{60}$.

5. C: 85% of a number means multiplying that number by 0.85. So, $0.85 \times 20 = \frac{85}{100} \times \frac{20}{1}$, which can be simplified to $\frac{17}{20} \times \frac{20}{1} = 17$.

6. A: Dividing by 98 can be approximated by dividing by 100, which would mean shifting the decimal point of the numerator to the left by 2. The result is 4.2 and rounds to 4.

7. C: 80 min. To solve the problem, a proportion is written consisting of ratios comparing distance and time. One way to set up the proportion is: $\frac{3}{48} = \frac{5}{x} \left(\frac{distance}{time} = \frac{distance}{time} \right)$ where x represents the unknown value of time. To solve a proportion, the ratios are cross-multiplied: $(3)(x) = (5)(48) \rightarrow 3x = 240$. The equation is solved by isolating the variable, or dividing by 3 on both sides, to produce $x = 80$.

8. A: The equation is *even* because $f(-x) = f(x)$. Plugging in a negative value will result in the same answer as when plugging in the positive of that same value. The function:

$$f(-2) = \frac{1}{2}(-2)^4 + 2(-2)^2 - 6 = 8 + 8 - 6 = 10$$

yields the same value as:

$$f(2) = \frac{1}{2}(2)^4 + 2(2)^2 - 6 = 8 + 8 - 6 = 10$$

9. C: The formula for continually compounded interest is $A = Pe^{rt}$. Plugging in the given values to find the total amount in the account yields the equation $A = 2000e^{0.05*8} = 2983.65$.

10. A: o. The core of the pattern consists of 4 items: ▲oo□. Therefore, the core repeats in multiples of 4, with the pattern starting over on the next step. The closest multiple of 4 to 42 is 40. Step 40 is the end of the core (□), so step 41 will start the core over (▲) and step 42 is o.

11. A: If each man gains 10 pounds, every original data point will increase by 10 pounds. Therefore, the man with the original median will still have the median value, but that value will increase by 10. The smallest value and largest value will also increase by 10 and, therefore, the difference between the two won't change. The range does not change in value and, thus, remains the same.

12. A: Let the unknown score be x. The average will be $\frac{5 \cdot 50 + 4 \cdot 70 + x}{10} = \frac{530 + x}{10} = 55$. Multiply both sides by 10 to get $530 + x = 550$, or $x = 20$.

13. C: Line graph. The scenario involves data consisting of two variables, month, and stock value. Box plots display data consisting of values for one variable. Therefore, a box plot is not an appropriate choice. Both line plots and circle graphs are used to display frequencies within categorical data. Neither can be used for the given scenario. Line graphs display two numerical variables on a coordinate grid and show trends among the variables.

14. C: A die has an equal chance for each outcome. Since it has six sides, each outcome has a probability of $\frac{1}{6}$. The chance of a 1 or a 2 is therefore $\frac{1}{6} + \frac{1}{6} = \frac{1}{3}$.

15. B: An equilateral triangle has three sides of equal length, so if the total perimeter is 18 feet, each side must be 6 feet long. A square with sides of 6 feet will have an area of $6^2 = 36$ square feet.

16. B: Each instance of x is replaced with a 2, and each instance of y is replaced with a 3 to get $2^2 - 2 \cdot 2 \cdot 3 + 2 \cdot 3^2 = 4 - 12 + 18 = 10$.

17. C: The area of the shaded region is the area of the square, minus the area of the circle. The area of the circle will be πr^2. The side of the square will be $2r$, so the area of the square will be $4r^2$. Therefore, the difference is $4r^2 - \pi r^2 = (4 - \pi)r^2$.

18. D: The expression is three times the sum of twice a number and 1, which is $3(2x + 1)$. Then, 6 is subtracted from this expression.

19: C. The two points are at -5 and 0 for the x-axis and at -3 and at -1 for y-axis respectively. Therefore, the two points have the coordinates of (-5, -3) and (0, -1).

20. A: The Pythagorean theorem states that for right triangles $c^2 = a^2 + b^2$, with c being the side opposite the 90° angle. Substituting 24 as a and 36 as b, the equation becomes $c^2 = 24^2 + 36^2 = 576 + 1296 = 1872$. The last step is to square both sides to remove the exponent, $c = \sqrt{1872} = 43.3$.

21. B: The formula for the volume of a cube is $V = s^3$. Substitute the side length of $7in$ to get $V = 7^3 = 343in^3$.

22. A: Figure out which is largest by looking at the first non-zero digits. Choice B's first non-zero digit is in the hundredths place. The other three all have non-zero digits in the tenths place, so it must be A, C, or D. Of these, A has the largest first non-zero digit.

23. C: 40N would be 4000% of N. It's possible to check that each of the others is actually 40% of N.

24. B: Instead of multiplying these out, the product can be estimated by using $18 \times 10 = 180$. The error here should be lower than 15, since it is rounded to the nearest integer, and the numbers add to something less than 30.

25. A: These numbers to improper fractions: $\frac{11}{3} - \frac{9}{5}$. Take 15 as a common denominator: $\frac{11}{3} - \frac{9}{5} =: \frac{55}{15} - \frac{27}{15} = \frac{28}{15} = 1\frac{13}{15}$ (when rewritten to get rid of the partial fraction).

26. B: $4\frac{1}{3} + 3\frac{3}{4} = 4 + 3 + \frac{1}{3} + \frac{3}{4} = 7 + \frac{1}{3} + \frac{3}{4}$. Adding the fractions gives $\frac{1}{3} + \frac{3}{4} = \frac{4}{12} + \frac{9}{12} = \frac{13}{12} = 1 + \frac{1}{12}$. Thus, $7 + \frac{1}{3} + \frac{3}{4} = 7 + 1 + \frac{1}{12} = 8\frac{1}{12}$.

27. C: The average is calculated by adding all six numbers, then dividing by 6. The first five numbers have a sum of 25. If the total divided by 6 is equal to 6, then the total itself must be 36. The sixth number must be 36 − 25 = 11.

28. B: Multiplying by 10^{-3} means moving the decimal point three places to the left, putting in zeroes as necessary.

29. B: $\frac{5}{2} \div \frac{1}{3} = \frac{5}{2} \times \frac{3}{1} = \frac{15}{2} = 7.5$.

30. A: The total fraction taken up by green and red shirts will be $\frac{1}{3} + \frac{2}{5} = \frac{5}{15} + \frac{6}{15} = \frac{11}{15}$. The remaining fraction is $1 - \frac{11}{15} = \frac{15}{15} - \frac{11}{15} = \frac{4}{15}$.

31. B: 93/8

The original number was 11 5/8. Multiply the denominator by the whole number portion. Add the numerator and put the total over the original denominator.

$$\frac{(8 \times 11) + 5}{8} = \frac{93}{8}$$

32. B: 8.1

To round 8.067 to the nearest tenths, use the digit in the hundredths.

6 in the hundredths is greater than 5, so round up in the tenths.

8.067

0 becomes a 1.

8.1

33. B: To simplify the given equation, the first step is to make all exponents positive by moving them to the opposite place in the fraction. This expression becomes:

$$\frac{4b^3 b^2}{a^1 a^4} * \frac{3a}{b}$$

Then the rules for exponents can be used to simplify. Multiplying the same bases means the exponents can be added. Dividing the same bases means the exponents are subtracted.

34. B: The car is traveling at a speed of twenty meters per second. On the interval from one to three seconds, the position changes by forty meters. By making this change in position over time into a rate, the speed becomes forty meters in two seconds or twenty meters in one second.

35. A: Finding the product means distributing one polynomial over the other so that each term in the first is multiplied by each term in the second. Then, like terms can be collected. Multiplying the factors yields the expression:

$$20x^3 + 4x^2 + 24x - 40x^2 - 8x - 48$$

Collecting like terms means adding the x^2 terms and adding the x terms. The final answer after simplifying the expression is:

$$20x^3 - 36x^2 + 16x - 48$$

36. B: The equation can be solved by factoring the numerator into $(x + 6)(x - 5)$. Since that same factor $(x - 5)$ exists on top and bottom, that factor cancels. This leaves the equation $x + 6 = 11$. Solving the equation gives the answer $x = 5$. When this value is plugged into the equation, it yields a zero in the denominator of the fraction. Since this is undefined, there is no solution.

37. B: Each instance of x is replaced with a 2, and each instance of y is replaced with a 3 to get $2^2 - 2 \cdot 2 \cdot 3 + 2 \cdot 3^2 = 4 - 12 + 18 = 10$.

38. A: To expand a squared binomial, it's necessary use the *First, Inner, Outer, Last Method*.

$(2x - 4y)^2 = 2x \cdot 2x + 2x(-4y) + (-4y)(2x) + (-4y)(-4y) = 4x^2 - 8xy - 8xy + 16y^2 = 4x^2 - 16xy + 16y^2$.

39. B: The y-intercept of an equation is found where the x-value is zero. Plugging zero into the equation for x, the first two terms cancel out, leaving -4.

40. C: The equation $x = 3$ is not a function because it does not pass the vertical line test. This test is made from the definition of a function, where each x-value must be mapped to one and only one y-value. This equation is a vertical line, so the x-value of 3 is mapped with an infinite number of y-values.

41. A: This answer is correct because $(2 + 2i)(2 - 2i)$, using the FOIL method is:

$$4 - 4i + 4i - 4i^2 = 8$$

Choice *B* is not the answer because there is no *i* in the final answer, since the *i*'s cancel out in the FOIL. Choice *C*, 4, is not the final answer because we add $4 + 4$ in the end to equal 8. Choice *D*, 4i, is not the final answer because there is neither a 4 nor an *i* in the final answer.

42. D: Multiply the top and the bottom by $(2 + 2i)$, the conjugate, to arrive at $\frac{8i}{8}$, which cancels to *i*.

Choice *A* is not the answer because the 8's cancel out. Choice *B* is not the answer because the 8's cancel out. Choice *C* is not the answer because 2 is not left, but 8 is.

43. D: The expression is three times the sum of twice a number and 1, which is $3(2x + 1)$. Then, 6 is subtracted from this expression.

44. D: There are two ways to approach this problem. Each value can be substituted into each equation. A can be eliminated, since $4^2 + 16 = 32$. Choice B can be eliminated, since $4^2 + 4 \cdot 4 - 4 = 28$. C can be eliminated, since $4^2 - 2 \cdot 4 - 2 = 6$. But, plugging in either value into $x^2 - 16$, which gives $(\pm 4)^2 - 16 = 16 - 16 = 0$.

45. A: Parallel lines have the same slope. The slope of C can be seen to be 1/3 by dividing both sides by 3. For E, divide both sides by 2 and see the slope is 3/2. The others are in standard form $Ax + By = C$, for which the slope is given by $\frac{-A}{B}$. The slope of A is 3, the slope of B is 4. The slope of D is 1.

46. B: The slope will be given by $\frac{1-0}{2-0} = \frac{1}{2}$. The y-intercept will be 0, since it passes through the origin. Using slope-intercept form, the equation for this line is $y = \frac{1}{2}x$.

47. D: The first field has an area of 1000 feet, so the length of one side is $\sqrt{1000} = 10\sqrt{10}$. Since there are four sides to a square, the total perimeter is $40\sqrt{10}$. The second square has an area of 10 square feet, so the length of one side is $\sqrt{10}$, and the total perimeter is $4\sqrt{10}$. Adding these together gives $40\sqrt{10} + 4\sqrt{10} = (40 + 4)\sqrt{10} = 44\sqrt{10}$.

48. C: If $\log_{10} x = 2$, then $10^2 = x$, which equals 100.

49. C: The $(3x + 1)$ can be factored to get $(2x - 5)(3x + 1)$.

50. D: Because the coefficient of x^2 is negative, this function has a graph that is a parabola that opens downward. Therefore, it will be greater than 0 between its real roots, if it has any. Checking the discriminant, the result is $1^2 - 4(-3)(-8) = 1 - 96 = -95$. Since the discriminant is negative, this equation has no real solutions. Since this has no real roots, it must be always positive or always negative. Its graph opens downward, so it has at least some negative values. That means it is always negative. Thus, it is bigger than zero for no real numbers.

51. B: The number of ways to order n objects is given by the product $\binom{n}{1}\binom{n-1}{1} \dots \binom{1}{1}$. This is $\binom{3}{1}\binom{2}{1}\binom{1}{1} = \frac{3!}{1!2!} \cdot \frac{2!}{1!1!} \cdot \frac{1!}{1!1!}$. 1! is just 1, and the 2! in the numerator and denominator will cancel one another, with a result of $3! = 3 \cdot 2 \cdot 1 = 6$.

52. C: Janice will be choosing 4 employees out of a set of 6 applicants, so this will be given by the choice function. The following equation shows the choice function worked out: $\binom{6}{4} = \frac{6!}{4!(6-4)!} = \frac{6!}{4!(2)!} = \frac{6 \cdot 5 \cdot 4 \cdot 3 \cdot 2 \cdot 1}{4 \cdot 3 \cdot 2 \cdot 1 \cdot 2 \cdot 1} = \frac{6 \cdot 5}{2} = 15$.

53. D: The volume of a cube is the length of the side cubed, and 5 centimeters cubed is 125 cm³. Choice A is not the correct answer because that is 2×5 centimeters. Choice B is not the correct answer because that is 3×5 centimeters. Choice C is not the correct answer because that is 5×10 centimeters.

54. B: The volume of a rectangular prism is the $length \times width \times height$, and $3cm \times 5cm \times 11cm$ is 165 cm³. Choice A is not the correct answer because that is $3cm + 5cm + 11cm$. Choice C is not the

correct answer because that is 15^2. Choice *D* is not the correct answer because that is
$3cm \times 5cm \times 10cm$.

55. C: The volume of a cylinder is $\pi r^2 h$, and $\pi \times 6^2 \times 2$ is $72\,\pi$ cm³. Choice *A* is not the correct answer because that is only $6^2 \times \pi$. Choice *B* is not the correct answer because that is $2^2 \times 6 \times \pi$. Choice *D* is not the correct answer because that is $2^3 \times 6 \times \pi$.

56. C: The volume of a pyramid is $(length \times width \times height)$, divided by 3, and $(6 \times 6 \times 9)$, divided by 3 is 108 in³. Choice *A* is incorrect because 324 in³ is $(length \times width \times height)$ without dividing by 3. Choice *B* is incorrect because 6 is used for height instead of 9 $((6 \times 6 \times 6)$ divided by 3) to get 72 in³. Choice *D* is incorrect because 18 in³ is (6×9), divided by 3 and leaving out a 6.

57. C: The formula for the volume of a sphere is $\frac{4}{3}\pi r^3$, and $\frac{4}{3} \times \pi \times 6^3$ is $288\,\pi$ in³. Choice *A* is not the correct answer because that is 12^2. Choice *B* is not the correct answer because that is 10^2, and Choice *D* is not the correct answer because that is $6 \times 2 \times 10$.

58. A: This answer is correct because $100 - 64$ is 36, and taking the square root of 36 is 6. Choice *B* is not the correct answer because that is $10 + 8$. Choice *C* is not the correct answer because that is 8×10. Choice *D* is also not the correct answer because there is no reason to arrive at that number.

59. A: This answer is correct because $(3 + 3i)(3 - 3i)$, using the FOIL method is: $9 - 9i + 9i - 9i2 = 18$. Choice *B* is not the answer because there is no *i* in the final answer, since the *i*'s cancel out in the FOIL. Choice *C* is not the final answer because you have to add the two 9s together in the FOIL method. Choice *D* is not the final answer because there is neither a 9 nor an *i* in the final answer.

60. C: First, factor out the 3's: $\frac{1+i}{1-i}$. Then multiply top and bottom by that conjugate: $1 + i \rightarrow \frac{1+2i+i^2}{1-i^2}$. Since *i* is the square root of -1, this goes to: $\frac{1+2i+(-1)}{1-(-1)}$. This equates to $\frac{2i}{2}$. Cancelling out the 2's leaves *i*. Choice *A* is not the correct answer because that only represents the denominator that is part of a fraction that needs to be simplified. Choice *B* is not the correct answer because that only represents the numerator that is part of a fraction that needs to be simplified. Choice *D* is not the final answer because it shows only part of the result from the FOIL method.

61. B: The formula for the length of an arc is $(central\ angle) \times (2\pi r) = (arc\ length) \times (360°)$, and $(72°)(2\pi 20) = (arc\ length) \times (360°)$, which reduces to 4π inches. Choice *A* is not the answer because it is double the correct arc length. Choice *C* is not correct since it is half of the correct arc length. Choice *D* is not the correct answer because it shows that the canceling of the numbers is not correct.

62. D: The formula for the area of the circle is πr^2 and 5^2 is 25. Choice *A* is not the correct answer because that would be 2 times the radius. Choice *B* is not the correct answer because that would be 5×3. Choice *C* is not the correct answer because that would be 2^2 times the radius.

FREE Test Taking Tips DVD Offer

To help us better serve you, we have developed a Test Taking Tips DVD that we would like to give you for FREE. **This DVD covers world-class test taking tips that you can use to be even more successful when you are taking your test.**

All that we ask is that you email us your feedback about your study guide. Please let us know what you thought about it – whether that is good, bad or indifferent.

To get your **FREE Test Taking Tips DVD**, email freedvd@studyguideteam.com with "FREE DVD" in the subject line and the following information in the body of the email:

  a. The title of your study guide.

  b. Your product rating on a scale of 1-5, with 5 being the highest rating.

  c. Your feedback about the study guide. What did you think of it?

  d. Your full name and shipping address to send your free DVD.

If you have any questions or concerns, please don't hesitate to contact us at freedvd@studyguideteam.com.

Thanks again!

69650076R00066

Made in the USA
Middletown, DE
08 April 2018